THE
VICTORIAN KITCHEN
GARDEN

The Victorian Kitchen Garden

JENNIFER DAVIES

It cannot be that the kitchen-garden can fairly be considered
either the least important or the easiest to manage or learn.
It takes in a far wider range of society than any other department.
Neither the prince or the peasant can neglect it with impunity.

The Gardener, January 1869

W·W·NORTON & COMPANY
New York   London

I am sincerely grateful to my colleagues Brian Hawkins, who helped make the idea become reality, Christopher Lewis, who saw the project through its early stages, and Keith Sheather, who produced the television series.

I am also grateful for the invaluable advice given by George Gilbert of Long Ashton Research Station and by Brian Halliwell, Assistant Curator of the Royal Gardens at Kew.

Thanks must also go to Dr Brent Elliott and Barbara Collecott of the Royal Horticultural Society Library for their kind help.

Finally I would like to thank the book's three editors, Sheila Elkin, Valerie Buckingham and Nina Shandloff, and, for her care over the design, Linda Blakemore.

PICTURE CREDITS

Black and white photographs page 11 National Monuments Record; pages 13 top, 19, 27, 86 and 139 BBC (John Perkins); page 13 bottom Harry Dodson; pages 16, 17, 76, 100, 103, 117 and 131 Jennifer Davies; pages 25 and 142 Brian Hawkins; page 28 The Trustees of the Chatsworth Settlement; page 30 BBC Hulton Picture Library; page 46 BBC (Robert Hill); page 51 Rothamstead Experimental Station; page 55 Jack Knight Photography; pages 140 and 146 (both) Countess of Beauchamp, MBE, K[1], and Trustees of the Madresfield Estate.

Colour photographs 1 Martin Dohrn; 2, 3 and 4 Jack Knight Photography; 5, 7, 8 and 33 Jennifer Davies; 6, 14 and 15 Howard Blakemore; 9, 11, 18, 19, 23, 25, 30, 34, 35 and 36 BBC (John Perkins); 10, 12, 13, 20, 21, 22, 24, 26, 27, 28, 29 and 31 BBC (Robert Hill); 16, 17 and 32 Brian Hawkins.

Map page 15 Line and Line; *chart* pages 66 and 67 Jennifer Davies and Brian Haynes; *engravings* reproduced from contemporary Victorian gardening books.

By arrangement with BBC Books
A division of BBC Enterprises Ltd

© Jennifer Davies 1987

First American edition, 1988

ISBN 0-393-02539-X

W. W. Norton & Company, Inc., 500 Fifth Avenue, New York, NY 10110
W. W. Norton & Company, Ltd., 37 Great Russell Street, London WC1B 3NU

Printed in Great Britain

1 2 3 4 5 6 7 8 9 0

CONTENTS

·

FOREWORD
•
by Peter Thoday

'BBC Bristol – Miss Jennifer Davies – please contact.' A telephone message like that to a University Department of Horticulture usually means a five-minute chat on topics such as giant hogweed or the current thinking on acid rain – but not this time. Within minutes the standard opening, 'We are seeking information on', became, 'I am very interested in' and then, 'I want to know more about . . . where can I read details of . . .' Clearly, this was no ordinary 'reporter'. This person was a self-motivated student of Victorian gardening, and one who had already done a tremendous amount of homework. But what an unusual subject, certainly not one you would find in any exam syllabus today. So, why ring me? Well, yes, my students and I had been involved in some work in the ruins of a walled garden on the South Glamorgan Heritage Coast, but I thought Jennifer must have been pretty desperate to be following such slim leads. Months later I learned that Jennifer had been somewhat surprised that a Senior Lecturer in a University Horticultural Department that prides itself on studying today's and tomorrow's cultivation techniques was happily rambling on about forcing seakale and hand-pollinating melons. It was not long before she prised the truth out of me. It was not my academic self that was talking, it was my boyhood as the son of a head gardener, brought up among more than 100 varieties of apples and sleeping at nights in an air-raid shelter constructed from a rhubarb-forcing house. From Jennifer's first call I was hooked on the idea behind the series. It has been my great privilege to present the combined work of the production team, the camera crew and, of course, Harry the head gardener and Alison, his assistant.

I have never worked with such a committed group of people. Nothing but perfection was good enough for our producer Keith Sheather and cameraman Paul Morris and his colleagues. Of course, most of us could have been replaced, but it is my belief that we had in our company not one but two examples of a very rare phenomenon indeed: the irreplaceable person. I refer, of course, to Harry Dodson and Jennifer Davies. Their absence would, without doubt, have greatly diminished the quality of these programmes. Harry's contribution has been clearly recorded. Indeed, in a very real sense, he grew the pictures himself. Jennifer's contribution is not so obvious to the viewing public, but surely it must be evident to the readers of this book: this is a work of enthusiastic scholarship. But, just as the programmes could accommodate only a small part of the information found in this volume, so Jennifer has also had to leave unexplored here many of the topics she researched so well. Inevitably, the publisher's limit on the number of pages has taken over from the producer's stop-watch. I look forward to more on this subject in the future from her pen.

I must add a warning to amateur gardeners and professional horticulturists reading this book: take care. Jennifer reports on many old methods and Harry has experimented with a few for the television series. Some were zany, indeed some were contrary to our present understanding of plant growth. Others worked well. Regrettably, neither a television series nor a book of this nature is a suitable place to debate the scientific principles, if any, behind all the old recommendations and practices we unearthed. But what superb topics for horticultural student projects!

So, what are our conclusions at the end of this project? First, it has helped us all appreciate the origins of much of today's horticulture and respect the ingenuity and intelligence of last century's gardeners. The work-load required to produce high-quality products by traditional means has shown very clearly why so many people were needed to cultivate such small areas, but it has also given us a glimpse of how high the productivity was. And what of the vexed question of superior flavour from old varieties grown by traditional means? Well, certainly there is a variation in taste between varieties, and this century's plant breeders may in some cases have overlooked that; it is also possible to spoil flavour by bad husbandry. Nevertheless, I believe that the two overriding advantages the world of the walled garden had over today's retailers were that produce matured on the plant and was eaten fresh, often within an hour or so of harvest. I was struck by the excellence of old fruit varieties compared with the generally inferior standard of old vegetable and flower types.

So, I praise Jennifer for this book, my ancestors for their green-fingered intelligence, and I am more than thankful for the work of research stations and the twentieth-century sciences of crop protection and plant breeding! Finally, I wonder what will be said about us and our horticultural activities in a hundred years' time.

Peter Thoday, Bath 1986

CHAPTER ONE

·

The forgotten gardens and how one was rediscovered –
Harry tells the story of the syringe.

PERAMBULATING around stately houses, politely filing
behind muted but gawping queues, your rubber-soled summer
shoes squeaking on polished oak in a bright but faintly alarming
twentieth-century way, may not enhance the imaginative powers.

Here's the master bedroom with its white bath modestly shut into a
grand cupboard. The green and brown bachelor bedroom, a faded
nursery suite, the drawing-room with stiff *chaises-longues* and glass clusters dim from the lack of candlelight and, passing through the double
doors: the dining-room. Immaculate and empty, the last dinner invitation as yellow and lost as the grand menu card it had heralded . . .
and yet . . . and yet . . . pausing against the roped rail you realise that if
you had rustled into the room a hundred or more years ago, it wouldn't
have been to admire the painted cornucopias on the Royal Worcester
dinner-plates or the gleam of the mahogany flute-legged table – you
probably wouldn't have seen either. The table legs would have been
hidden under a white damask cloth and the plates covered with far
more beautiful a collection of fruit and vegetables than any porcelain
painter could match.

Among the forest of table palms there would be the opulence of the
fruit: peaches displayed as velvet pyramids set on beds of leaves, cone-
shaped spirals of cherries and currants with their stalks patiently and
modestly turned inwards. There would be dishes of apples beautiful in

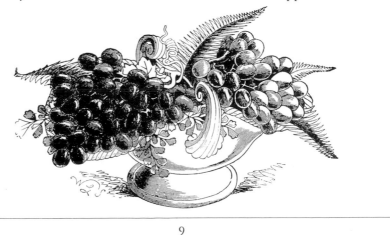

their diversity: russeted, large and red-flecked or small and golden yellow. Pears dappled like a trout's back and plums with a bloom as fragile as breath on a window, kept unsmudged by gentle gathering into a basket of nettles. The air would be pungent with the honey smell of ripe melons, handsome, smooth, cut at the peak of perfection, not a moment too soon or too late. There'd be a pineapple on a silver dish, so fresh that the top still gleamed with the humidity of the hothouse. And the *pièce de résistance*, cunningly rising from beneath the centre of the table, a small *living* vine heavy with bunches of grapes to be delicately picked at between courses. Courses which might include asparagus, tender early green peas, blanched seakale, cardoons, scorzonera and a host of forgotten delicious vegetables. The ghosts of lilies and orchids and Japanese chrysanthemums still linger in the empty grates, and the wide window sills support empty porcelain jardinières, once the home of fan palms and near neighbours of glass-cased pitcher plants.

The unknowing and unperceptive who hadn't sensed the phantom banquet and the heavy smell of orchids in the drawing-room would probably at this point make their way to the converted scullery and laundry-room for tea and home-made cakes. Others more energetic might wander round the formal gardens admiring bedding plants. The really adventurous and enlightened would set off for the outer limits of the pleasure grounds where, if they were lucky and brave enough to face the nettles and smothering brambles, they might be rewarded by finding the walls of that one-time most important, but now most neglected institution – the kitchen fruit and vegetable garden.

Tucked away from the visitors this once grand and immaculate status symbol of the nineteenth century is more than likely to be an embarrassment to its present-day owners. It is a Victorian legacy frequently kept behind locked doors, neglected, weed-choked and forgotten, a victim of twentieth-century economics and cheap imports. Yet in its heyday the walled kitchen garden would have ranked as one of the most important places on the estate.

Even distanced by neglect, it deserves to be remembered and admired as much as any of the silk-lined drawing-rooms or state bedrooms.

The area inside its walls was the hub which kept the house and grounds running. It was the inner sanctum for that most respected of men, the head gardener, who often had his house built into the garden wall. The head gardener and his staff were expected to supply the wealthy owner with a continuous and varied supply of fresh fruit, vegetables and flowers every day of the year.

From the walled garden came the best vegetables for the dining-room table and the choicest fruits for the dessert plates. Without the

Archive photographs showing kitchen gardens in full production are rare. This one shows the kitchen garden at Easton Neston, Northamptonshire

aid of modern-day appliances, the head gardener had to answer the imperious call for strawberries in winter and salads all the year round in sufficient quantity to cope with any number of unexpected house guests and their servants. The walled garden had also to provide exotic flowers for the table, often in colours to match the ladies' dresses, and to keep up a constant supply of palms and pot plants for the rest of the house. In addition, by ingenious methods involving lead evaporating trays and hotbeds under frames, the head gardener might be expected, despite the odds, to keep the lady of the house supplied with out-of-season lily of the valley and violets. Besides all this, every single one of the massive number of formal bedding-out plants which filled the borders in the pleasure grounds in summer had to be started, wintered and nurtured in the walled garden.

Although the walled kitchen garden is one of the oldest forms of garden, it seems that for a number of reasons the splendour within the four walls reached its zenith in Victorian times. It would be difficult to find so compact an area which so well reflects Victorian ideals: the quest for improvement, for one-upmanship, the inventiveness, the interest in science and the strict social hierarchy. Pull away the brambles and figuratively dig about a bit and the Victorian walled kitchen garden would tell a story probably more fascinating than the stately house it served.

There have been a great many television programmes which have looked at baronial halls, focused on inanimate expanses of Chippendale, or closed in on the ancestral silver. Why should we not, instead, take the cameras behind the sun-blistered paint of the kitchen garden doors and discover the delights of wrought-iron work, warm reflecting walls, interesting artefacts and the initiative and skills of the men who once worked there? It was their expertise that filled the tables with produce fine enough to meet any silver knife edge.

It was a nice idea, but painstaking searches revealed a major stumbling block. It was going to be extremely difficult to find a suitable walled kitchen garden. Well-meaning contacts and local history societies sent in long lists of possible sites. Visits revealed that many gardens were now bereft of all but their walls and formed grazing for merino sheep or friends' Shetland ponies. Others were so bramble-choked that an army of expert machete handlers would have made little impact. One had a swimming pool inextricably placed in it, another was now a maize field. A few, a brave few, capable of being counted on one hand, survived. Madresfield Court near Malvern in Worcestershire, Barrington Court in Somerset, Barleywood in Avon were still extant, but for the most part it seemed that the Victorian kitchen garden was lost before it could be rescued – had we left it too late?

It was at this point that I decided to turn to the other problem to be faced. To bring alive the Victorian garden it would be necessary to show the skills that were used. How were fruit and vegetables obtained out of season? How were houses of exotic fruit such as figs and nectarines 'managed'? How was the hardy walled fruit trained into the traditional espalier and fan shapes? We needed someone who had actually done it. Of course, fate would not thoughtfully provide us with a centenarian Victorian head gardener walking perfectly preserved from his fruit room but those familiar with the gardening world said that there was still a handful of men left who might be able to help. One was retired head gardener Harry Dodson, who lived at Chilton Gardens near Hungerford in Berkshire.

I met Harry Dodson on a cool October morning. Chilton Gardens wasn't difficult to find; the garden wall dominates the road which runs through the picturesque hamlet of Leverton. Opposite the wall the River Kennet ripples down into the village of Chilton Foliat. Perhaps I should have had an inkling of what I was going to find at Chilton when I saw the neat estate cottages, thatched and solid and peaceful, edging the green. At first sight Chilton would have fitted into a nineteenth-century pastoral drama. A long, low range of brick buildings flanked the back of the north wall of the garden. There were heaps of loam, dried leaves and sand in open-fronted buildings. Tucked up into the rafters were several age-greyed produce hampers and old wooden orchid boxes.

Above: Harry Dodson
Below: Harry as a boy in
the kitchen garden at
Selborne

Despite the cold wind, Harry Dodson met me in rolled-up shirt sleeves. He was tall and spare and, for someone credited with so much knowledge of the old ways, looked surprisingly young. Outside his office was a small white board: H. J. Dodson FRHS.

Inside, even a chair would have been an embarrassment. The place was built for work. There was just sufficient standing room for one person (a head gardener) to lean and write up accounts and orders at a plain counter top fixed to catch the light from a small barred window. Facing north, the room was sunless and the flagged floor made it distinctly chilly. Two things caught my eye. One was a pile of old account books which had been in the small dark office for so long that their marble-patterned backs were smudged with white mould; the other was the right-hand wall. It was cluttered with horticultural certificates. Even the dust and curling corners could not obliterate the embossed medals and important horticultural awards.

Yes, Harry Dodson remembered the old days of walled kitchen gardens and how things had been done. He'd been born on the Earl of Selborne's estate in Hampshire. As his father was dead, his mother's brother, Fred Norris, kept a kindly eye on him. Uncle Fred was head gardener to the Earl and Harry started off life toddling around the estate's walled kitchen garden. When he was thirteen the Countess of Selborne took him on to work as a garden boy under his uncle and paid him a penny-farthing an hour.

After Selborne came jobs in a number of estate gardens to provide the necessary rungs up the horticultural ladder, then in 1947 he came to Chilton as head gardener. He was twenty-seven and with a staff of nine gardeners was responsible for looking after the pleasure grounds, the vineries, peach, nectarine, melon and fig houses, and supplying vegetables, pot plants and cut flowers to the mansion. In 1956 he had been asked to join the Royal Horticultural Society's prestigious Fruit and Vegetable Committee which involved, and still involves, attending meetings at the headquarters in London and judging at their shows.

The world within the walled kitchen garden had been slow to change and many of the skills Harry had learned, such as successional sowing, fruit cultivation and forcing vegetables, had been handed down for generations. The aim of keeping the house well supplied with produce every day of the year despite the odds had remained the same, he felt, certainly up until the Second World War, and in some cases beyond.

We walked out of the office and towards one of the several tall doors which led into the garden. Harry explained that Chilton, like most large estate gardens, had for economic reasons altered over the past few years. The staff dwindled, the vines had been pulled out and finally the boiler which heated the glasshouses sprang a leak which proved difficult to repair. That, combined with the rising cost of oil, spelt the end of heating the houses and they had fallen cold for the first time since being built. After that it had been difficult to halt the general decline all round.

The garden door swung back: to our left was the end wall of a long line of glasshouses, to our right the high side wall which marked the beginning of another row. These had been the vineries, the nectarine and early and late peach houses. Opposite stretched the remains of a four-acre (1.6-hectare) garden which had necessarily lost its original layout in a mixture of decay and modernisation. We walked along the right-hand range of old glasshouses which spanned seventy feet (21 metres) ending against an east-facing wall. At the near end of this wall a brick archway led out of the large garden.

Stepping through the arch, the shock came. In front of us, battered and crumbling but with the bones still intact, was what I had spent weeks searching for – a walled fruit and vegetable garden. Small enough to be refurbished, complete with Victorian glasshouses, and on the doorstep of one of the few men left whose past experience could help remake and rediscover the ingenuity within and peculiar beauty of the walled kitchen garden.

The garden we were looking at appeared to be just over an acre (0.5 hectare). It sloped southwards. At the top end the glasshouses ran horizontally with the one large house in the centre built outwards to make a squat 'T' shape. Below the glasshouses and midway down the garden was a double row of coldframes. Closer examination of the frames caused the feeling of euphoria to drop considerably. Only a few splintered fragments of glass remained and many of the tops had disappeared as well. Every border was thick with couch grass and nettles. The box edging to the side borders was depressingly erratic. In places it had grown high and rangy, bushes were far neighbours rather than close family. For long stretches it had disappeared altogether.

Behind the glasshouses the warm pink surface of the south-facing wall was a historic record. Hundreds of nail holes pitted the bricks, a legacy of the careful training of generations of past peach and nectarine trees. Not one tree remained. On the surrounding walls a few apple and pear trees showed vestiges of the training they'd received in the days when Harry had had time and staff but for the most part they were straggly and overgrown.

Any gravel that might have once covered the paths had long since disappeared under mud and weeds. Recent rain had made a small pool in the far left-hand corner of the garden. Missing bricks in the steps leading up to the glasshouses made the approach difficult but it was

Right: Sketch plan showing the layout of the kitchen gardens at Chilton

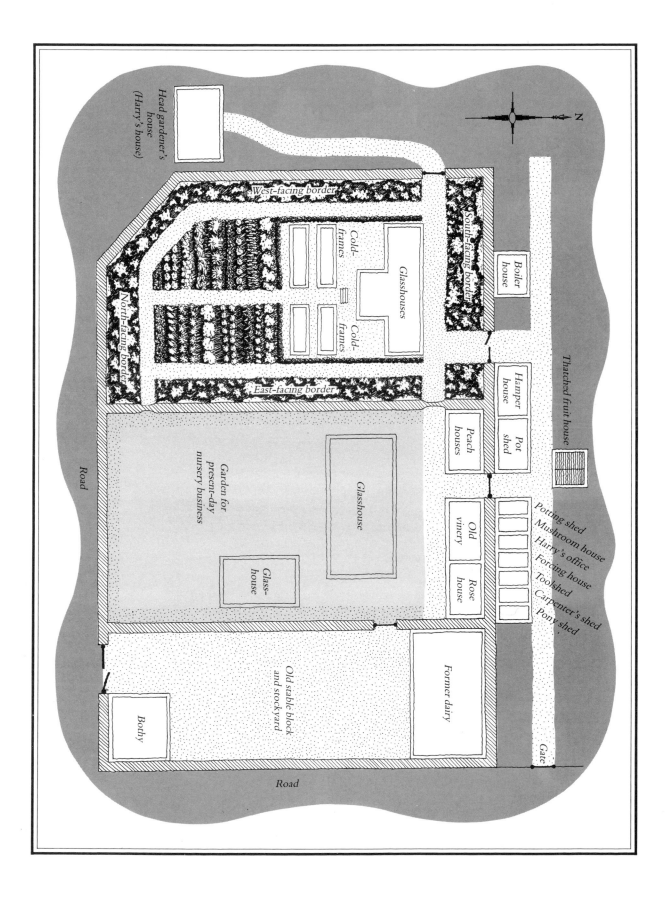

Head gardener's house (Harry's house)

West-facing border

South-facing border

North-facing border

Cold-frames

Cold-frames

Glasshouses

East-facing border

Boiler house

Hamper house

Pot shed

Peach houses

Old vinery

Rose house

Thatched fruit house

Potting shed

Mushroom house

Harry's office

Forcing house

Toolshed

Carpenter's shed

Pony shed

Garden for present-day nursery business

Glasshouse

Glass-house

Former dairy

Old stable block and stockyard

Bothy

Road

Road

Gate

N

Left and right: The depressing sight of the unrestored garden at Chilton, showing neglected glasshouses, broken cold-frames and overgrown paths and borders

worth the effort. Despite broken guttering and paintless grey wood, the houses still retained most of their glass. Inside the large central house, small ornate wrought-iron posts rose from a red-tiled floor to support iron benches which ran down either side of the house. Ornate wrought-iron supports spanned the roofs and a network of Victorian heating pipes, in some cases complete with lead evaporating trays, skirted the borders.

A poignant reminder of forgotten summer days lay in a corner. It was a water syringe, eighteen inches (45 centimetres) of fluted brass and still in working order. Formerly, garden boys would have spent many weary hours walking up and down fruit houses spraying trees and floors with such a syringe in an effort to maintain the correct humidity.

Harry picked up the syringe. It was the same, he said, to garden boys as left-handed hammers were to apprentices of other trades. A new boy would have been given this sort of syringe and told to dip it into the stone water troughs in the hothouses and begin the chore of spraying. The boy would have got as far as filling the syringe but then invariably would have found that, pump as he might, no spray of water obligingly emitted from the other end, a worrying fact if he were faced with a fifty-foot (15-metre) range of rapidly drying vegetation. Inevitably most boys returned dismally to the fruit foreman. After feigning surprise that such a simple task had caused a problem, the foreman would, with a flourish, take the syringe, place the forefinger of one hand against the end nozzle and, pumping with the other, produce a perfectly powered spray and at the same time demonstrate how sensitive movement of this useful digital valve could vary direction and intensity.

Besides the syringe, other fragments of summer days were less well-preserved. The thin wooden strips of shading blinds, once part of neat continuous cascades, lay mouldering in fragments, some bits still capable of providing shade but none long enough to hoist on the iron roof pulleys.

Out of the glasshouses, we walked back down the steps, passed under a rusty ornamental arch, a reminder of a row of arches which once spanned the central pathway, and made our way to Harry's office. Now came the delicate question. In addition to offering horticultural advice, would Harry be prepared to let us take over the walled garden – bearing in mind it might be a lengthy project – and, more to the point, did he think that the garden *could* be restored to the layout and excellence it might have displayed a hundred years or so ago?

Harry picked up one of the old account books. It was dated about the turn of the century and the first pages listed the produce sent up to the mansion in January: artichokes, chicory, asparagus, dandelion, seakale, endive, celery and, from the fruit store, pears for stewing. Some of these tender winter vegetables had fallen out of fashion but Harry thought that there was no reason why, using the right care and resurrecting the old terracotta forcing pots and lantern cloches, we couldn't bring them back to the walled garden. The entry for March was definitely daunting, it showed strawberries, early beans and salads. For the summer months there were peaches, nectarines, figs, hothouse and coldframe cucumbers and melons, gooseberries, currants, plums, cherries . . . an endless list.

Given the present state of the garden it wouldn't be easy. The best help we could give Harry, apart from supplying advice from various historians and nineteenth-century gardening manuals, was one enthusiastic horticultural student, a far cry from the days of dozens of gardeners.

We might make a pig's ear of the whole project. It was a considerable challenge but Harry Dodson picked up the gauntlet – or should it have been gardening glove? Like us, he saw it as an opportunity to make a visual record of the old methods and skills and at the same time celebrate the Victorian fruit and vegetable varieties before many of them disappeared for ever.

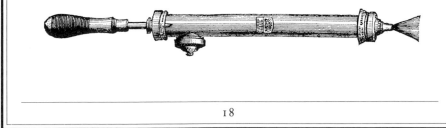

CHAPTER TWO

•

Finding apple trees and their histories – Mr Snow's theory on turf –
Paving stones, an unearthed mystery.

WHEN we began the first major task of restoration, choosing the varieties of fruit trees, it was late autumn and cold. The most important were apple trees since these would thrive against any of the four walls and could be trained to spread along post and rails around the vegetable borders.

Old catalogues showed extensive lists; one for the 1880s boasted 500 different varieties of apple available in their nursery. Although many of those being sold today have stood the test of time and are legacies from the preceding century, it was interesting to see that a great number of the apples had actually been introduced during the Victorian period. One of the reasons for this might have been that at the beginning of the nineteenth century there was great concern about the state of the apple trees in the country. Many trees were old, diseased and giving poor crops. To make matters worse, some infected apple trees were brought over from France to a nursery in Chiswick in London. Perhaps no one noticed that these particular trees had a fine white cottony substance lodged in the crevices of their bark. Had anyone looked closely it might have become apparent that the substance was made up of a mass of insects whose bodies were covered with white strands. The insects cause American Blight and, left untreated, they would quickly kill a tree by attacking both its roots and branches. The aphid spread to other London nurseries and as these nurseries supplied most of the country it wasn't long before American Blight had spread to all the main apple-growing areas.

To combat the situation, the recently set up Royal Horticultural Society began to look at scientific ways of improving pest controls and at the same time new and healthy varieties were brought in from the Continent. Nurserymen also experimented with breeding their own varieties. All this, combined with the general Victorian love of collecting and desire for something new in the gardens, helped to swell the number of varieties introduced, especially during the latter end of the nineteenth century.

We could find no records that stretched far enough back to show which specific apple varieties had been grown in the walled garden at Chilton, so we set about drawing up our own list. We needed both dessert and culinary apples; some which would ripen early in the season and some late, and some which would store well so that the supply would be stretched as far into winter as possible. Other considerations were flavour, appearance and apples with interesting histories.

The next step was to check the old nursery lists against modern catalogues and see which Victorian varieties were still available. Most of today's nurseries had very few of the old names listed but after a lot of searching we came across one or two which still grew an encouragingly full list of old varieties. We did, however, have a problem. Not only had our trees to be of the right period but we wanted young trees on which the nursery had started to train the branches. We needed the beginnings of the old-style espalier and fan shapes which we could continue to train and which would look so beautiful spread against the garden walls. Telephone calls to the nurseries selling the old varieties brought disappointing news. Hardly any trained their trees anymore. They found it too time-consuming. To obtain an espaliered two-tier tree, that is one which has two sets of horizontal branches placed neatly and symmetrically, takes up to five years of preparation – the branches require careful pruning and pinioning to straight canes. The general feeling was that today's customers had neither the time nor knowledge to continue the training, so it was easier and more profitable to sell bush and small standard trees. This seriously curtailed our list. Compared with the rich variety shown in Robert Hogg's *Fruit Manual* for 1884 it was pitiable. Mr Hogg was an editor of the *Journal of Horticulture* and his 750-page *Fruit Manual*, now avidly sought by antiquarian booksellers, describes in detail all the fruits and fruit trees in Great Britain. A good third of Mr Hogg's book is devoted solely to apple varieties being grown at the time; he ends the section with a list of what he considered to be the best dessert and culinary apples. He selected 147 dessert and 106 culinary varieties. Our list, owing to unavailability and further restriction over training, finally numbered fourteen varieties of dessert apples and a mere six culinary.

Most easily available was Cox's Orange Pippin which we chose for its fame and flavour. Now grown all over the world, the apple was raised in 1825 by Mr Richard Cox, a retired brewer of Colnbrook in Buckinghamshire. It is said to have been grown from the pip of a Ribston Pippin. The Ribston itself at that time was a famous old apple. It had originated from pips sent from Rouen in Normandy to Ribston Hall, Yorkshire, in 1707. The seedling which sprang from the Ribston

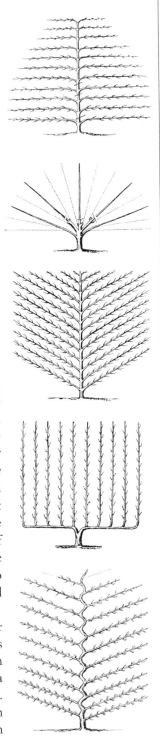

Left: Methods of training fruit trees shown in the Gardener's Assistant of 1859 (from top): horizontal, fan, oblique, upright and wavy or curvilinear

pip was grafted by the gardener at Mr Cox's home, Lawn Cottage, and the first Cox's Orange Pippin grew in the vegetable garden there.

Cox's Orange Pippin hit the headlines in 1857. Shock was expressed when the judges at that year's Grand Fruit Exhibition passed over its famous father the Ribston Pippin and chose instead the new, unknown offspring which was destined to become England's most famous apple. Mr Cox's home eventually became the headquarters for an engineering firm and a recent visit to search for it proved disappointing. Not a brick remains, where the house once stood is a row of modern semi-detacheds and what was once the gardens is now partly a primary school and partly an industrial estate.

As the Cox is to dessert apples, so the Bramley is to culinary apples. So we put Bramley's Seedling on the list. It is a large, handsome apple and, like the Cox's Orange Pippin, trees are still readily available. At one time every cottage garden had a Bramley. Robert Hogg called it a 'very valuable cooking apple' with flesh of 'a yellowish tinge, tender, and with a fine brisk acidity'. He says that the apple was sent to him by a nursery firm called Merryweather. This gives the cue for an interesting story.

Merryweather's, who today still have a nursery at Southwell in Nottinghamshire, exhibited the apple in 1876 calling it Bramley's Seedling after the butcher Matthew Bramley who raised it in his garden at Southwell. No one questioned this until some years ago when research showed that in fact the apple was much earlier in origin and not raised by Mr Bramley at all. The true originator of the apple was Miss Mary Ann Brailsford who, in about 1809 when she was eighteen years old, sowed some pips in a flower pot, put the resulting seedling in her garden and went away to get married, leaving the tree to grow to maturity. In 1846 Mr Matthew Bramley bought the Brailsford house which by then, presumably, had a large and fruitful apple tree in the garden. Sometime later Merryweather's discovered the apple, were told that it came from Mr Bramley's garden and called it 'Bramley's Seedling'; subsequently poor Miss Brailsford's claim to fame remained lost in confusion for over a hundred years.

The other culinary apples we listed were Lane's Prince Albert originally raised in 1840; Newton Wonder raised in 1887; a good late cooker raised in 1851 Lord Derby; Warner's King and Golden Noble.

Among the dessert apples we chose Irish Peach, which was introduced from Ireland in 1820 and described by Robert Hogg as 'an early dessert apple of the finest quality ... it is most beautiful, and certainly one of the most excellent summer apples'; Devonshire Quarrenden, another early cropper but a much older apple, dating back to 1678.

Ashmead's Kernel was chosen for its exquisite flavour, again an apple popular in Victorian times but much earlier in origin, having been raised by a Doctor Ashmead of Gloucester in 1700. We added Worcester Pearmain because it serves as pollinator for Cox's Orange and was mentioned in an early Chilton garden account book. The apple was raised by a Mr Hale of Swan Pool near Worcester and introduced in 1874. Pitmaston Pine Apple was chosen for its beautiful russeted bright yellow skin. It had originated at Pitmaston, near Worcester, in 1785. An additional benefit was the apple's reputed rich, distinctive flavour and a cropping season that stretched from September to December. Another late variety added was the old Blenheim Orange, doubly valuable because it can be used for either cooking or dessert.

There was one particular apple that had been mentioned frequently in the old gardening manuals. It has a pleasing down-to-earth name, the Maltster. Hogg's *Fruit Manual* described it as an excellent culinary apple with flesh that was 'yellow, tender, sweet and agreeably flavoured'. It was certainly an apple to have in the garden. However, close scrutiny of every current catalogue did not reveal a single Maltster. It seemed that one might have enjoyed its delights in 1830, and no doubt for some considerable time after, but its pleasures were definitely denied those of us in the latter end of the twentieth century. In short, it had deceased and departed, seemingly for ever. I write seemingly, for one Maltster still lived. It is, no doubt, unless there are a few lingering in forgotten gardens, the only Maltster left in the world and it is in the National Fruit Trials' Apple Collection.

The collection is part of the busy Ministry of Agriculture Experimental Horticultural Station, Brogdale, which lies just outside the town of Faversham in Kent. The apples are kept as a genebank for breeders and also serve as a reference for identifying varieties. Brogdale's main task, however, is coping with the problems of today's commercial fruit industry, answering their enquiries and carrying out trials to evaluate new fruit varieties. In order to see the Apple Collection it is necessary to make an appointment.

When the trees are bearing fruit this living museum is an astonishing and beautiful sight. There are almost 2000 different varieties, all colours, shapes and sizes. There is the peculiar-shaped Cat's Head; the massive Twenty Ouncer; the small pinky-yellow Brookes's; delicately striped Hoary Morning; and the odd raised seam of Winter Banana. There is the vivid splash of Scarlet Nonpareil; slender, drooping Lady's Fingers; and many, many more. There are apples that the Romans probably knew, some certainly grown in the Middle Ages and a host of others, some so new that as yet they are known only by numbers.

I had foolishly imagined that all the trees would be bent and venerable: not a bit of it. There is row upon row of short, young, healthy trees, each labelled, clear evidence that our fruit legacy is being kept alive by careful and periodic grafting on to new root-stock.

The Maltster was there, alive and well and sandwiched between Malden Wonder and Milton. After due admiration of such a unique specimen, Brogdale very kindly gave us permission to go back in March the following year in order to take a graft from it for our garden. Like Mary Ann Brailsford and her misnamed Bramley, we might never see the tree come to maturity but at least the Maltster would be out in the world again.

That was a date for the following spring but it was still late autumn and time was running out. If the fruit trees we had chosen from the various nurseries were to make any growth worth looking at, we had to get them planted as soon as possible. Although there was no great number of trees, because of the scarcity of some of the old varieties it had been necessary to order just one or two from nurseries around the country. By lorry and van the precious deliveries began to arrive at Chilton. As well as the apples, there were two peach trees, two nectarines, one apricot, one greengage, several cherry and pear trees.

As we wanted to prepare the intended site for the fruit trees carefully, giving thought to what part of the garden would best suit each, Harry prepared a temporary resting place for them. Heeling them in, he called it. He dug a deep furrow in one of the overgrown borders and as each tree arrived, laid it obliquely with its roots well into the furrow, carefully banking up loose soil around the roots to prevent them drying out. Beneath the weeds, the soil in the garden was good but there was a nagging doubt. Some of the old trees which used to spread against the walls might have died from disease, and disease can linger on in the soil for years. We decided it was safer to dig out a fair depth for each tree and fill it with good topsoil from outside the garden which we knew was free from contamination.

Robert Thompson's extremely hefty *Gardener's Assistant*, published in 1859, advocated good loam for fruit tree borders and a depth of soil of three feet (1 metre). He gave fifteen feet (5 metres) from wall to path as an average width for a fruit border for gardens between one and two acres (0.5 to 1 hectare). The south-facing border against the north wall was certainly fifteen feet (5 metres) in width but the west-, east- and north-facing borders around the rest of the garden varied in size, some had been eroded by bits of pathway or just seemed to have shrunk inexplicably with time. It was more sensible to construct the south-facing border larger than the others so that there was a maximum amount of soil for crops in the warmest part of the garden. We weren't too dismayed about the narrower borders as the soil would be good and on the strength of that felt they certainly fell in line with Thompson's maxim that 'the width of the border is the extent necessary for affording the roots sufficient nourishment'. On the subject of nourishment, Shirley Hibberd, another gardening sage of 1863, assured us in his *Profitable Gardening* that we were better off without manure as 'in any good soil that will produce a cabbage, the apple will thrive better without manure than with it'. We believed that the soil would pass the cabbage test, so began to dig the first hole. It was traditionally in the south-facing border where the more tender fruits such as peaches, apricots and nectarines were planted. We planned to space the trees, ten in all, twelve feet (4 metres) apart, from one end of the wall to the other.

Lord Napier stood patiently by, a two-year-old nectarine with a healthy root system and young branches trained out from birth into an attractive fan shape.

Nectarine

Digging went smoothly, it was obvious that the garden had been well tilled in the past, the spade was just reaching the required three-foot (1-metre) depth when, with a scraping jar, it hit a large stone. Scratching around the surface of the stone to expose a finger hold to lever it out proved frustrating. The stone was very large, in fact, the more the spade scraped away the soil, the more the stone's surface seemed to spread. What we'd struck turned out to be a flagstone measuring approximately three feet (1 metre) square. It was a great nuisance and exceedingly heavy to lift clear of the hole. Once it was out, the next stage, if we were to follow our Victorian predecessors as closely as possible, was to fill the bottom of the hole with bits of turf cut off a nearby piece of pasture. The *Gardener's Assistant* quoted advice given in the *Gardeners' Chronicle* by a Mr Snow of Swinton Park in Yorkshire in 1846. Mr Snow had said:

I do not mean to assert that fruit trees will not grow in other materials than turf, I have tried various soils and compounds, and some with fair success, but I never by such methods produced quantity, size or flavour. I believe turf procured from a pasture to contain properties adapted to the wants of trees, which artificial substitutes do not possess and I have always found that, in turf, the trees 'fibre' more, ramifying through in all directions. More moderate sized and fruitful wood is also formed.

It was an interesting theory and certainly very long term as Mr Snow believed that once done, the turves need not be renewed for twenty or thirty years. The merits he gave overcame the feelings of chagrin at having to give temporary alopecia to what had been quite an attractive piece of green pasture in an orchard next to the garden. Mr Snow was, however, a thorough man and by some 150 years he'd anticipated our feelings and further mollified them, by going on to say:

I am aware that many are of the opinion that injury is done to a pasture by paring off the turf; but I am of belief that it is mostly to the eye, and that only temporarily; and surely nobody who takes a delight in a garden would ... think anything too good which was essential, more especially when counterbalanced by the production of good-flavoured fruit, which, whether growing or placed on the table, is a source of pride and pleasure to all parties; but reverse the picture, and with fruit not fit to be eaten or looked at; observe the painful feelings of all – the gardener the great sufferer, although the fault lies beyond his control. To produce good fruit, good means and good materials, must be employed; and for fruit borders, my conviction is that nothing is better than green turf.

Who were we to argue with that?

So into the bottom of the hole went the turf, followed by Lord Napier and a fair quantity of healthy soil carefully trodden firmly around him. Our first tree planted! It was a significant moment but not one we could linger over as several more holes needed to be dug.

Twelve paces on we began the hole for tree number two, a Hale's Early peach. Three feet (1 metre) down the spade came to a jarring halt – another wretched paving stone buried flat and broad. Harry scratched his head, it was odd, he vaguely remembered finding the same

The old paving stone comes to light

thing when he was a lad working for Lady Katherine Ashburnham and digging in the very old fruit borders at Ashburnham Place. It seemed too much of a coincidence. Was there a purpose to the buried paving stones? Indeed there was, and further research revealed it.

The stones were laid to cope with a problem the Victorians had but which doesn't bother us today. Nineteenth-century fruit trees were produced from seedling root-stocks – just ordinary apple trees which had seeded well and gave a good healthy root-stock on which to graft. The problem was that once planted these trees, like any ordinary tree, would put down a deep tap root and grow up to a great height so that all the goodness went into making leaves and branches and not much into making fruit.

It was noticed, however, that there was one area of the country where this problem did not occur: a thoughtful Mr Keane is quoted by Robert Thompson as observing that in a particular part of Kent: 'Fruit trees of all sorts flourish and produce abundantly; even peach and pear trees of the most delicate kinds grow with the greatest luxuriance ...' Mr Keane attributed this strange phenomenon to the soil in which the trees grew. It was known as stone-shatter, and was sandy loam mixed with small bits of Kentish ragstone forming a depth of 'two to six inches on top of solid rock'. Mr Keane believed that this 'naturally hard bottom' slowed the trees' growth and that their tissues became 'perfectly organised as growth proceeds'. He recommended the practice of paving the bottom of fruit borders because, where there was bad subsoil, this stopped injurious substances affecting the trees' roots and where there was good soil it limited the supply of nourishment and stopped the tree producing 'a more luxuriant growth than the climate could render perfect'. Another method of trying to combat this problem was lifting fruit trees regularly and cutting back the roots to encourage them to make more fibrous roots near the surface.

That we don't have to tackle tap roots today is credit to the scientists at the East Malling Fruit Research Station in Kent. In the early part of this century they developed trees which had much smaller and more fibrous roots and which eventually became known as dwarfing stock. Now, wherever you go, practically every tree is on dwarfing stock; small, easy to harvest and a good fruit bearer. Not many people realise that it was Britain who first gave the world dwarfing stock.

Our Hale's Early peach, although a Victorian variety, had been grafted on to dwarf root-stock so we didn't need the paving stone but leaned it temporarily and reverently against the wall. No longer a nuisance, it was instead archaeological evidence of our predecessors' ingenuity.

CHAPTER THREE

•

The importance of manners – Where a journeyman slept –
Harry tells the borage story – Paxton, who came in the 'flood time'.

Alison training the fan-shaped peach trees by 'tying-in' new growth with strips of bast

ALISON MACKENZIE arrived in January 1985. She had been a student at Hadley Horticultural College in Kent and had come to give Harry full-time help. Alison's assistance was much needed; if she in turn gained something from the restoration work and from learning the old gardening techniques Harry still practised it would be a bonus. Harry's techniques, not on any modern college curriculum, were those which had been handed down, man to boy, for generations, in the exclusive institution of the walled fruit and vegetable garden.

It was an institution that we could only partly recreate with the old produce varieties and methods, we could never hope to restore the social hierarchy and traditional work-force the garden would have seen a century earlier.

Certainly there would have been no girl apprentices. If a woman were employed, she would probably have been a weeding woman, paid a pittance to spend hours on all fours scratching weeds out of the gravel paths with the spiked tips of leather gloves. This was in order that every path would be immaculate for the owner and his family and friends when they walked around on tours of inspection. Women might also have been given casual work, picking off caterpillars or hoeing, but it was a man's world and the god within it was not the master of the house but the head gardener.

Within the confines of the walled garden – and indeed the rest of his domain which would include the pleasure grounds – the head gardener ruled supreme. His standing was probably on a par with the status of the highest house servant, the butler, and in some ways it went beyond that. Gardening, with its attendant emphasis on science and taming nature, was considered a gentlemanly pursuit; good head gardeners were keenly sought and an employer often regarded his head gardener as a respected equal. Throughout the Victorian era, explorers and collectors were bringing new and exciting plants into the country and experiments were being made to introduce new fruit varieties. It was a form of snobbery to have a plant or fruit that your neighbour didn't possess and some head gardeners managed to take this one-upmanship

a step further. They developed new varieties and named them after the garden in which they served or, as in the case of the 'Lady Henniker' apple introduced in 1840, as a compliment to a member of their employer's family.

Garden staff at Chatsworth House in Derbyshire

Such niceties were equally practised by the employer and his family, who would not dream of cutting a single flower or picking any of the fruit without the consent of the head gardener. The confines of the walled garden were extra security for the choicest fruits and the head gardener kept them under close scrutiny, generally an easy task as his house was often built into the walls of the garden. His house was rent free and this, plus the perks he received either in beer money or from selling off surplus produce from the garden, augmented his wages. In 1868 Mr William Cox, head gardener to Madresfield Court and originator of the famous grape 'Madresfield Court', earned £25 a half-year with two shillings (10p) a week beer money for looking after gardens and grounds of considerable size. Fifteen years later his successor, William Crump, who had previously been head gardener to the Duke of Marlborough at Blenheim Palace in Oxfordshire, was paid double the money, £50, for a half-year.

An advertisement in the *Gardeners' Chronicle* for January 1870 illustrates another source of revenue:

To Parents and Guardians

WANTED, an active, intelligent, well-educated Youth, about 15, as an apprentice in a large Private Garden. Moderate Premium.

A.B., Post Office, Bury St Edmunds.

This head gardener was seeking a pupil who would pay him a premium for instruction received. It was a system that attracted criticism. Many thought it unfair that boys on private estates had to pay for the garden doors to be opened to them whereas their town cousins who lived near market gardens 'get everything opened, and yet give nothing'.

A crock boy might earn six shillings (30p) a week and out of that have to pay a shilling (5p) for his lodgings and two shillings (10p) premium to the head gardener. Head gardeners defended the system by saying that boys were a great deal of trouble at first and that in later years they would reap the benefit of the instruction.

The gulf between the garden apprentice and the head gardener was awesome. A head gardener wore a suit and top hat and did very little physical labour. He supervised the laying-out of the bedding plants in the pleasure grounds, issued orders, inspected the garden and hired and fired garden staff. The hiring of staff was very much a word-of-mouth affair. Head gardeners often met at horticultural shows or corresponded with each other, and it was the practice with most of them to keep a list of suitable men likely to need placing.

Harry confirmed that this method went on certainly up until the Second World War. Harry's uncle, Fred Norris, head gardener to the Earl of Selborne, helped Harry to get his early garden jobs then, when Harry was seventeen, urged him to apply to work under Mr Thomas Tomalin, head gardener to the Earl of Bessborough at Stansted Park in West Sussex. Mr Tomalin was, says Harry, well-known at the time and a great contributor to horticultural journals. It was Mr Tomalin's practice to tell his gardeners that if they suited they would stay with him for eighteen months, at the end of which time he would place them in one of the best gardens in the country. This had the twofold benefit of keeping the staff young and keen and the wages bill low!

Rising from crock boy to head gardener was a thorough and lengthy process. A crock boy would progress, usually when he was seventeen, to the post of improver journeyman, still learning his trade but not so green as an apprentice and often having moved on to another garden. Improver journeymen lived, like all unmarried male garden staff, in plain spartan-like cottages known as bothies. Although head gardeners' houses were generally built into the face of the warm south wall of the

Left: A garden boy receives instruction in the pleasure grounds
Below: Bothy staff at Blenheim Palace in Oxfordshire circa 1870

kitchen garden with their front doors opening out into the garden, no employer would waste the valuable space of the south wall on under-gardeners. Bothies were often built on the reverse, and cold, north side of the same wall and faced on to the complex of sheds, manure heaps and forcing frames outside the garden wall.

The plainness of bothies might have been considerably if rather peculiarly enhanced had one Victorian contributor to the *Gardener* had his wish. He suggested having WHERE THERE'S A WILL, THERE'S A WAY printed in letters of gold and fastened to every bothy in the country. This maxim was indicative of the great Victorian quest for improvement. Young gardeners were urged to study the remarkable phenomena continually occurring in the vegetable kingdom around them and to remember that the greatest facility that ever entered the garden was 'noticing':

Noticing while you learn to 'wield the ponderous spade' with dexterity, remember that 'elegance, chief grace the garden shows, is the fair result of thought' and try at the same time to penetrate into the fibre of the phenomena which are presented to you every day in the garden.

Reading was also recommended as a way of yielding profitable results. But all this reading and thinking had to be done after the twelve-hour working day because 'no honest or truly earnest man will let study interfere with the right performance of any portion of an actual duty'. As improver journeymen shared bedrooms in the bothy and had to rise early in the morning, any one of them burning the midnight oil over textbooks must have been exceedingly unpopular!

This preoccupation with education extended into another aspect which was the matter of manners, considered important as gardeners had to come into contact with people of taste. The 'Squire's Gardener', writing in the *Gardener* in September 1869, commented:

Modesty is characteristic of superior ability. Neatness in appearance and a prompt and ready address are always pleasing to employers. Snobbishness and foppery are utterly contemptible in the eyes of those whose bread we eat, or who are our superiors in position, and who look at us from an elevated social stand-point.

After a couple of years, during which time improver journeymen had presumably improved sufficiently in gardening techniques and maybe in manners, they could drop the prefix and become journeymen. As an additional benefit of their new status, journeymen were entitled to a bedroom of their own in the bothy. From journeyman the next step was to foreman. Foremen were directly responsible to the head gardener and there was a foreman in charge of each department of the garden. A man could gain valuable experience by becoming foreman of the fruit under glass in one establishment, then perhaps moving on to another garden to become foreman of the vegetable garden or pleasure grounds. After working in several different departments as a foreman, a man could consider himself sufficiently qualified to apply for a head gardener's post.

The foreman of the vegetable garden was responsible for making up the produce order for the kitchens. He sent his garden boy up to the house every morning to collect a written order from the cook. Often the foreman or head gardener sent up word to the cook that a particular vegetable was at its best. The boy ran back with the cook's order and the foreman made up the vegetables and fresh herbs into two baskets which the boy then hooked on to a shoulder yoke and carried carefully up to the kitchens.

Harry remembered that in his very young days he had an additional morning task. If he managed to get up to the butler's pantry by eleven o'clock with a bunch of fresh borage and a young cucumber for the claret cup then the butler rewarded him with a piece of cake. The cucumber was to decorate the sides of the silver cup and the blue

Borage flower

flowers of the herb, borage, to float on top of the claret. Borage is historically attributed with the power to give men merry hearts and drive away sadness; no doubt the claret helped as well.

The pleasures of claret cups and produce baskets have receded into dimly pleasant memories but one man still carries on a vestige of the tradition. Dennis Hopkins, head gardener to the Duke of Devonshire, makes his way each morning through the dim passages which lead from the Chatsworth courtyard to the kitchens. Although the four large formal kitchen gardens, which covered almost seven acres (2.8 hectares) at Chatsworth, have long since fallen into disuse, Mr Hopkins still grows vegetables for the house. Each day he recommends to the cook which vegetables are at their best and carries freshly made-up produce baskets to the kitchen. Mr Hopkins also performs two other tasks which were traditionally the province of head gardeners. He decorates the rooms, window sills and grates with cut flowers and pot plants from the garden hothouses and he 'dresses' the dinner-table with flowers. The flowers for the rooms might well have, as in the case of the blue and white drawing-room, to blend in with the décor of the room and, with equal precision, the flowers for the dinner-table might well have to match the colours of the ladies' dresses.

No doubt these were all tasks performed by Mr Hopkins' famous predecessor Joseph Paxton, head gardener to the sixth Duke of Devonshire. Paxton, later Sir Joseph, was an extraordinary man: gardener, architect and Member of Parliament. Probably his greatest achievement was his design of the huge glass building which housed the 1851 Great Exhibition and became known as the Crystal Palace. He based his design on the structure he had built at Chatsworth for the famous water-lily *Victoria regia* with its leaves big enough to carry a child. Once, when reminded of his achievements, Paxton replied:

I happened to come in the flood-time, and by the energies that God had given me, and by the able assistance of many eminent men, I have been enabled to carry out these great works, and to attain the position I now occupy.

There is no doubt that one of those 'eminent men' was the sixth Duke of Devonshire and it is interesting to note that both men, great in their separate ways, thought of the less fortunate. In 1865 the Duke was President of the Gardeners' Royal Benevolent Institution and Joseph Paxton was the Chairman.

The Institution had been formed in 1839 and subscriptions went towards helping impoverished aged gardeners or their widows. In 1856 the subscription was a guinea (£1.05) a year and from it each year twenty men received £16 and eleven women £12 each. Sir Joseph

Chatsworth House in an engraving from the Journal of Horticulture, 1874

Paxton, speaking at the Institution's Thirteenth Anniversary Dinner, drew attention to the unfair smallness of gardeners' wages compared with mechanics and artisans – who were receiving £2 a week and upwards. He urged gentlemen to look at the list of those they employed in places of trust and told them that they would find that the gardener was always the worst paid. As a consequence of this, later in life gardeners were driven to seek aid from the Institution.

If mechanics and artisans could earn £2 a week and upwards in 1856, it is a sad and telling fact that almost forty years later, in 1894, the Chilton Garden Wage Book gives the average wage of the gardeners at Chilton as fourteen shillings (70p) a week, with three, perhaps apprentice boys, earning only six shillings (30p) a week.

The Gardeners' Royal Benevolent Institution still exists but in 1959 it changed the Victorian-sounding 'Institution' to 'Society'. To be eligible for a Society pension, gardeners, nurserymen and seedsmen have to have been in their profession for twenty years and head gardeners for ten. Harry Dodson sits on the committee which allocates pensions. Four times a year he travels to London to sift through applications and put into action aims set almost a century and a half ago.

CHAPTER FOUR

•

Walls, paths and the vexed question of edging –
Behind the north wall – Heating boilers and a cow vinery.

'Plant trees in autumn and command them to grow;
plant in spring and beg them to grow.'

DESPITE the adage we didn't actually command the apples, pears, plums, cherries, peaches, nectarines, greengage and one apricot we had planted at Chilton to grow, well certainly not out loud, but bearing it in mind we hurried on with the task. With planting safely accomplished and the winter weather set in there was time to reflect on the geography and layout of the garden.

It was set about half a mile (0·8 kilometres) away from the mansion. Not untypical, for although early kitchen gardens were built close to the house many, particularly during the nineteenth century, were moved out into the grounds. Some owners considered that they obstructed the view from the house and a move also gave the opportunity to rebuild on a much grander scale. William Cox of Madresfield Court recounted in an 1875 edition of the *Gardeners' Chronicle* how nine years previously, on the accession of the then Earl Beauchamp, the Madresfield kitchen garden had been moved 'because it was 'very old, badly situated, and unequal to the probable requirements of a large establishment'.

Our Chilton garden was built next to the old stable block. Again, typical and sensible, for it meant a ready supply of horse manure was close at hand. As the present stable yard was neat and clean and given over to small craft workshops without a hint of manure in sight, it meant that instead of wheeling steaming barrow-loads through the door in the adjoining wall, we would have to rely on the good graces of the estate farm manager and his modern tractor and trailer. This was probably a relief to our student, Alison. The stable yard did, however, with its red brick set off by slatted white wooden air vents, make a pleasing addition to the walled garden complex.

The shape of the garden was more square than rectangular with the far right-hand corner curving into the north-facing wall. Deciding the shape and angle of the walls for kitchen gardens used to be a mixture of taste and science. Often measurements were meticulously taken to find the meridian line and the walls intended to run north to south built to correspond with it. Lines at right angles to the meridian gave the direction for the walls running east and west. Great care was taken to note where and when the sun was hottest and how long it would stay on a wall. In some parts of the country the sun was directly on the warm south-facing wall at eleven am and hot enough to ripen peaches and nectarines. In colder parts of the country the sun wasn't at its warmest until one pm. The south wall was built at a slight angle to accommodate this. Most gardeners considered that a straight rectangular shape was the best form for a kitchen garden, favouring a long south-facing wall with a corresponding north-facing wall and shorter east- and west-facing walls.

Below left: A table recording the results of nineteenth-century experiments to ascertain the sun's heat on garden walls
Below: The ideal shape and size advocated for a kitchen garden

Time.	Force of Sun's Rays.
$9\frac{1}{2}$ A.M.	32°
$10\frac{1}{2}$,,	46
$11\frac{1}{2}$,,	55
$12\frac{1}{2}$,,	63
$1\frac{1}{2}$ P.M.	65
$2\frac{1}{2}$,,	63
$3\frac{1}{2}$,,	58
$4\frac{1}{2}$,,	49
$5\frac{1}{2}$,,	35
$7\frac{1}{2}$,,	29

Progress of Solar Radiation from Morning to Evening, in June, upon an average of five experiments.

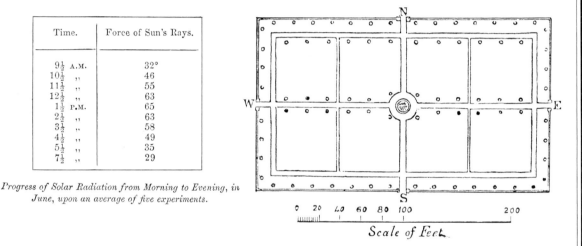

Scale of Feet.

The value and warmth of the walls could be lost if cold winds managed to get into the garden. Once inside and unable to drift away, as they would on open ground, the trapped winds could eddy around inside the walls and injure both fruit and vegetables. To stop this happening, plantations of tall, quick-growing trees such as Italian poplars, spruces and larches were planted as wind-breaks outside the north, north-west and north-east sides of the garden walls. There was still a row of tall trees including larches behind the north wall at Chilton and Harry remembered tall trees being behind the other walls which had been cut down when old age had made them unsafe. Since their demise, the temperature in the garden had fallen considerably. The height of the walls at Chilton was imposing, at twelve feet (4 metres), with, at a rough calculation, enough bricks in them to build thirty-two semi-detached houses. A particularly clever piece of bricklaying had coped with the standard southward slope and the not-so-standard peculiar curving west wall.

Below: Cross section of wall showing width and coping-stone

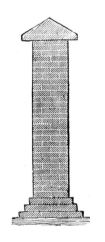

To enclose a garden with walls was to lay out a considerable expense. Robert Thompson in his *Gardener's Assistant*, 1878 edition, made the calculation that to enclose an acre of land with a wall fifteen feet (5 metres) high, estimating the brickwork at £12 a rod (5 metres), would cost £552. For four acres (1·6 hectares), the size needed to maintain supplies to a large country house, the cost would have been £1104. To that had to be added the price of glasshouses (still quite considerable despite the removal in 1845 of the crippling tax on glass), a heating system for the glasshouses and the cost of other garden buildings.

Within the walls, the accepted form of layout was to have borders beneath each wall with a pathway running around the garden separating the wall borders from the large central plot. As at Chilton, the middle plot generally had a central pathway running north to south. Most other large kitchen gardens also had a pathway running across the garden west to east making four central plots instead of two as we had at Chilton. In these larger gardens, where the two paths met at the centre of the garden it was thought desirable to have sufficient room for a horse and cart to turn round. However, even with our single central path we still had room for a heaped wheelbarrow to turn comfortably, depending on who was wheeling it.

Although the top surface of the paths at Chilton had disappeared under mud and weed, some stretches still had the traditional camber to help water drain from the centre of the path. The recommended way of making a garden path a hundred years ago was to lay a nine-inch (23-cm) bed of broken granite and top it off with two inches (5 cm) of coarse gravel and an inch (2·5 cm) of fine gravel. As the old manuals said, it would make an excellent walk such as could not be surpassed for a kitchen garden. Probably an indisputable fact, yet although we were striving for excellence at Chilton the present-day price for sufficient granite and gravel to surface all the paths in the garden was prohibitive. Scratching the surface of the old paths revealed a form of shingle which, when brought to the surface, rolled and added to, we decided would look attractive and do us as well, if not as elegantly, as gravel.

There were certainly no volunteers to act as weeding women with leathered talons, but we did intend to search out the iron foot-scrapers – if they still existed – and place them as they would have been, at the junction of every border with a path so that after we had finished digging or hoeing our boots could be scraped clean and the pathways kept unsullied.

The concept of immaculacy within the garden was reflected in what Victorian garden journalists called a 'difficult subject'. 'Nothing', wrote Mr Shirley Hibberd in 1877, 'contributes in a more decisive way to the enjoyment as well as the usefulness of a garden as well-made walks and neat edgings.' It was the neat edgings which caused the concern. Some gardeners favoured living plants such as strawberries, chives, chamomile or parsley; others thought that these harboured slugs, impeded cultivation and spread untidily across the paths. Newly-fashionable clay tiles were held to be the answer but Mr Hibberd considered that, although nine-tenths of them answered the edgings question admirably, when there was heavy rain followed by hard frost, then 'they split into fragments and have to be swept up as rubbish'.

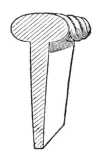

Clay edging tile

Most gardeners fell back on the old favourite, small box bushes. William Cobbett gave the following delightfully lyrical tribute to box edging in his *English Gardener*:

The box is at once the most efficient of all possible things and the prettiest plant that can possibly be conceived; the colour of its leaf; the form of its leaf; its docility as to height; width; and shape; the compactness of its little branches; its great durability as a plant; its thriving in all sorts of soils, and in all sorts of aspects; its freshness under the hottest sun, and its defiance of all shade and all drip; these are beauties and qualities, which, for ages upon ages, have marked it out as the chosen plant for this very important purpose ... and if there be a more neat and beautiful thing than this in the world, all that I can say, is that I never saw that thing.

As mentioned earlier, the paths at Chilton had been edged with box but instead of the proper height of seven inches (18 cm) the box had become massive overgrown clumps interspersed with yawning gaps. Finding a large number of good-quality box plants proved difficult. We discovered that even nurseries which were box specialists and displayed at Chelsea didn't keep vast amounts of plants. Enquiries about where we could obtain specimens as splendid as the ones exhibited at shows revealed that these displays were kept carefully trimmed and the same plants reappeared each year. It seems that box is far more popular in continental gardens than in this country. Eventually the nursery we had asked to help us tracked down a consignment in Holland.

The plants were good quality and arrived in bundles of thirty. With the aid of a twine line following the edge of the pathway, Harry set about putting them in. Instead of planting each separately, he dug out a long straight trench about four inches (10 cm) deep and, following the line of the twine and pathway, took the bundle and played out the plants into the trench, each one fairly close to the other. He brought the loose earth from the top of the trench back down around the box stems with his hand, firming as he went along. As soon as two sides to a path were planted we began to appreciate William Cobbett's description. Neatness and beauty were slowly returning to Chilton.

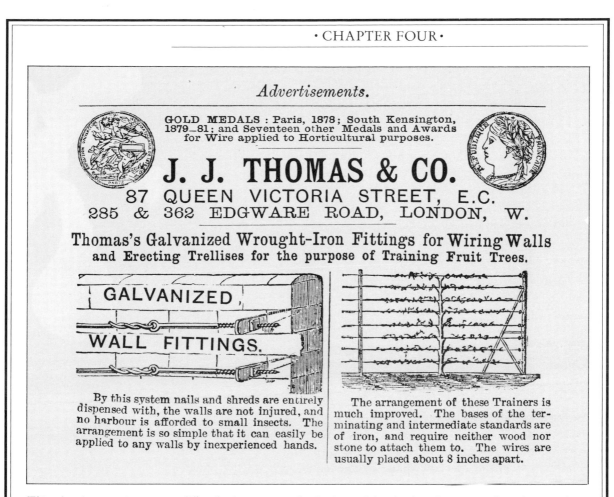

This advertisement shows that the old system of tagging and nailing was gradually being replaced by wires and nails

The fruit trees we had planted in the border seemed to have taken and Alison pruned back the few old fan-shaped pear trees which still lingered in the garden. We had decided to resuscitate these because they were good old Victorian varieties such as Louise Bonne of Jersey, William's *Bon Chrétien* and the long-keeping Joséphine de Malines.

Following sense and tradition, we had planted our fan-trained peaches, nectarines, apricots and early plums against the north wall on its warm, south-facing aspect. The east-facing wall with its fairly indifferent aspect was traditionally the place for fruits which ripened in full summer and autumn – pears, cherries and plums. Against the west-facing wall we had planted Victoria and Denniston's Superb plums; Early Rivers and Governor Wood cherries; pears and a few choice dessert apples including Cox's Orange Pippin and the later-ripening Sturmer Pippin. At the bottom of the garden, the north-facing wall was always planted with morello cherries and plums. Our north-facing wall also had a few old pear trees which Harry said did well despite the cold aspect.

At one time the outside of the garden walls at Chilton had also been planted with fruit, for the reverse of the cold wall was another valuable, warm, south-facing surface, which reflected heat and helped to ripen fruit. It was generally the hardier fruit that was planted on the outside as there was too great a danger of unscrupulous 'scrumping' by passers-by to chance the choice fruit outside the walls.

Many gardeners, with an eye to making the garden as productive as possible, also planted fruit, generally apples and pears, at the edges of the vegetable borders. Standard trees would have taken up too much room and shaded the valuable vegetable ground beneath, so it was customary to erect post and rails and tie the fruit trees along them, either as attractive horizontally-branched espaliers, or as cordons. Cordons were trees trained by removing all the lateral branches so that the fruit clustered around the straight main stem. They could be upright but many gardeners favoured having them sloping, a method known as the oblique cordon. Cordons and espaliers formed a productive and attractive border, the horizontal branches could be as much as forty-two feet (13 metres) wide yet low enough to escape wind damage and make harvesting easy. Another old method of combining beauty with bounty was to intersect the edges of the vegetable plot with pyramid trees. This was a French method of training and was usually applied to pear trees, pruning them until they were cone-shaped. Some gardeners even managed to train their red currants into pyramids. It was ideal for kitchen gardens for, as well as being decorative, a well-cultivated pyramid would throw no shade, give a gallon (4·5 cubic decimetres) of fruit and would take up only a square yard (0·8 square metre) of valuable ground.

Although we did not aspire to pyramids, we decided to put post and rails at the corner of one vegetable border and along the side of the path which ran horizontally between the glasshouses and coldframes. Along the rails we planted espalier apple trees, both dessert and culinary. To form a blossom arch in spring and a fruit canopy in autumn, cordons of Ashmead's Kernel apples and William's *Bon Chrétian* pears were planted and trained across the iron hoops which spanned the central path.

With the walled fruit making headway, the box edging planted along the paths and our post and rails bearing embryo culinary apples, even despite the overgrown plots of land, the garden began to give an exciting hint of what it might eventually become.

Smooth paths, bountiful fruit trees and verdant vegetable borders, charming as they are to look at, do, however, rather like beautiful princesses, have the same basic needs as lesser breeds of their species.

Food, refuse and heating all originated out of sight behind the garden walls. Such places were never intended to be seen by visitors and only by the master of the house if he went on purpose to inspect them. E. S. Delamer in his *The Kitchen Garden* written in 1855 described them as:

Places which receive heaps of decaying leaves, manure, broken potsherds, prunings of trees, last year's raspberry canes, and the various other offal of a garden, which must be put somewhere, and are best out of sight. A tool house, a mushroom house, a root shed, a propagation pit and several other etcetera which are more useful than ornamental, may thus be made to retire behind the scenes to play their part when called upon, and not before.

One place which played its part behind the garden walls at Chilton was Harry's office. From there, proceeding behind the north wall, was first a benched vegetable store, no longer used to store vegetables but playing host to crates, boxes, balls of string and the general ephemera of past gardening days. Then came a mushroom house with mouldering matchboard insulation and faded pencil scratches above the remnants of beds, recording when each was spawned. A dark, stone-floored 'forcing-house', providing a place for winter vegetables, and a refuge to frostbitten gardeners, was next. Outside its walls the snows never lay long but ran into puddles in the pathway dividing the row of buildings from the sheltering plantation of high trees opposite. The forcing-house, cold and bare, had double rows of huge heating pipes lying like redundant rusting pythons around the base of the walls.

Next came the potting shed with its waist-high, broad stone bench; the space beneath divided into stone-walled compartments once filled with different mixtures of soil. Two soil sieves – one large and one small – hung, grey with dust, on the wall above the bench.

From the potting shed the row extended into an open-fronted building with a bench and a space in front, large enough for mixing loam, leaves, sand and manure. This was the pot shed, once the workplace of the humblest member of the garden staff, the crock boy. The crock boy's job was to collect and deliver pots to every department in the garden when needed and keep them stored in neat rows of size order. He had to wash out used pots and line the bottoms of pots ready to be used with 'crocks', bits of broken flowerpots. He was taught always to put in at least a couple of crocks which came from the curved tops of broken pots so that the drainage hole was properly bridged and didn't become blocked. Hanging in the pot shed was a piece of bamboo approximately twelve inches (30 cm) long with a cylindrical piece of hardwood attached horizontally to one end. This, said Harry, was the crock boy's hammer, an instrument of great antiquity which had been at the garden long before Harry's day. With it, each day the crock boy

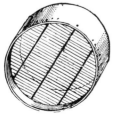

Above: Pyramid-trained tree
Below: Garden sieve

had to tap every potted-up plant in the garden. If the pot gave off a dull thud when struck, the plant was moist enough, if the pot 'rang' out then the plant needed watering. Woe betide the crock boy if the foreman did a spot check tap and found a pot which needed watering.

Set snugly into the row of trees opposite these places of potting and forcing was Chilton's *pièce de résistance* – the fruit store. In all my travels around walled gardens in various states and locations, I had never seen one so fine. It pointed out of the trees, end first, like a small cottage with an abundant thatch which had crept down the roof to cover all the walls right down to ground level. To be able to see inside, the fruit house had to be unlocked, for it was the garden's equivalent of a commercial strong room or bank vault and still locked by·habit, even though its contents were no longer as precious or numerous as they once had been.

Two steps led up to the door, placed high enough to keep out damp. Unlocked, it opened on to another door. This second door had fine wire mesh nailed over its top half and although less sturdy than the outer one, was also fitted with a strong, old-fashioned lock. Stepping down inside into the cool twilight the width of the walls of the building became apparent. Behind the outer thick thatching was a three-inch (8-cm) cavity and behind that an equally thick layer of cork, making the walls a good one foot (30 cm) thick. Insulating materials such as thatch and cork could keep the house at an even temperature, much desired in fruit stores. It had long been known that changes of temperature caused fruit to decay. There was one firmly-shuttered window, and to keep out the frost, wads of straw had been fixed tightly against its outer shutter. Harry said the window was kept closed and only opened when the fruit had been first picked. Then the straw was taken out and the window propped open. It was at this time too that the outer door was propped open exposing the wire-meshed inner door. Both door and window had stayed open for eighteen days to allow the newly-gathered fruit to 'sweat'.

Slatted wooden shelving ran along the sides of the house and rose in three widely spaced tiers in the centre. In all, the fruit house matched exactly the conditions the Victorian fruit expert M. Du Breuil attributed to a perfect fruitery: 'A temperature always equal, complete seclusion from light; no communication with the external atmosphere and a northern aspect on a dry foundation.' Added to which there was the bonus of a delightful lingering smell of apples – not ghosts of the past but coming from a small quantity of large, gently puckering, pinky yellow Peasgood's Nonsuch. The large culinary apples had been gathered by Harry earlier in the year and laid on a shelf near the door.

At the extreme end of the north wall, outwardly looking for all the world like another potting shed, was the boiler house. I suppose if I had possessed a rudimentary knowledge of physics, the shock would have been less. The floor just inside the boiler house door fell away into a fifteen-foot (5-metre) chasm. It was an organised fall, two sets of extremely rusty ladders providing access to the murky depths below. The boiler had been placed at such an astonishing depth to cope with a gravity problem. The ground in the kitchen garden, the other side of the wall, quite intentionally sloped downhill. This was so that the higher ground beneath the south-facing wall caught the warm sunshine. Unfortunately, this meant that the two glasshouses built almost half-way down the garden were six feet (2 metres) below the level of the garden wall. To send hot water to heat these houses efficiently and to get the water to return to the boiler, the early engineers had to sink the boiler as low as possible. Another reason for the extraordinary depth was the upright tubular boiler. Its defunct remains were partially bricked up but it was easy to see how much taller it would have been than the more convential horizontal-shaped boiler. Extra depth was necessary to compensate for this height. The boiler had been stoked with coke from the top. Propped in a corner, a legacy of horizontal boilers, were six-foot-long (2-metre) poles and scrapers once used to rake out the waste clinker, now as rusty as the descending ladders.

Weeks's Patent Upright Tubular Boiler

When Harry first came to Chilton Gardens there were two tubular boilers. One had to be kept going full tilt. It was stoked first thing in the morning, early afternoon, late afternoon, and on cold nights as late as nine o'clock to keep the heat up until morning. On Friday nights this boiler was allowed to go out and the other one was lit. Next morning the duty man cleaned out the cold one and set it ready to be lit on the following Friday night.

Heating glasshouses by hot water began to become popular in the 1830s. Before that time, houses had been heated by lighting furnaces which carried hot air and gases up flues along the front and back of the houses. It was an efficient but costly way of heating a large area of glasshouses. With the hot-water system, a furnace was lit beneath a boiler which was filled with water. Once hot, the water rose up a flow pipe and travelled through a network of iron pipes which ran around the glasshouses. The water then flowed back through a return pipe which entered the base of the boiler. When the return water, now considerably cooler, re-entered the boiler, it forced the much hotter water up through the flow pipe and so a circulation of hot water was kept going. To maintain a really good heat it was necessary to have a fast flow of hot water. Experiments were made to ascertain the rate of flow. The simplest way was to drop a piece of paper into a section of pipe and time its reappearance. Giving a boiler a steep return pipe helped to circulate the water around the glasshouses as rapidly as possible. Perhaps this was another reason for the depth of the boiler house at Chilton, although the tubular boiler was noted to have been the most powerful and most expensive of all the types of boiler on sale in the nineteenth century. On a tubular boiler, unlike its horizontal competitors (the saddle-shaped or cannon-shaped boilers), the surface exposed to the furnace was small. This resulted in fewer deposits of soot hampering efficiency. Also, a tubular boiler had no joints, so was not likely to spring a leak.

We could never afford to get the tubular boiler at Chilton running again even had it been repairable. The heat for our hothouse melons and cucumber would have to come from a more modern source. Before leaving the subject of the boiler house it is worth mentioning two interesting heating alternatives.

One was practised by a Mr Lawson of Tirydail near Llandrillo in 1852. Nothing so mundane as a boiler for Mr Lawson, he relied on animal heat. He had what he called a cow vinery. In it the cows were housed for the winter and, said Mr Lawson:

Very pretty they look with a row of chrysanthemums on the wall in front of them just coming into blossom ... we have laid planks across the tie beams and loaded them with pots of calceolarias, geraniums, strawberries, etc, etc, the vines have grown extremely well ...

The efficiency of the heat the cows produced was not doubted. What troubled the gardening experts of the day was the dust created by the cows, presumably from the straw beneath. Mr Lawson admitted it was a bit of a problem but thought he made it worse by ordering that the cows be currycombed and brushed.

Another heating system was patented by a Mr Pannell. It was a complicated network of tanks and pipes with wonderful capabilities. It could provide a moist bottom heat for pineapples and cucumbers one minute or a dry bottom heat for melons the next. Its price was eight guineas (£8.40) plus a third-class rail fare from London and the cost of Mr Pannell's refreshments.

CHAPTER FIVE

·

*Tools – Trenching – The magnitude of manure and the success of a
gentleman who 'went into' it.*

*Above: The Desideratum
Watering Can
Below: Mr Pullinger's
Patent Sulphurator,
invented in 1870
Below right: The London
Treaded Spade*

S AMUEL BEETON (publisher of *Beeton's Guides to Good Gardening* and husband of the cook Mrs Beeton) takes 173 pages to
describe 'Garden tools, implements and appliances required for
working the soil, measurements, sowing, planting, transplanting,
potting and watering.' Mr Beeton, sensible husband of sensible wife,
does not branch into the huge range of ingeniously dotty nineteenth-
century garden appliances which were regularly invented, reported and
wilted without trace, for instance, the Desideratum Watering Can
invented by the Reverend Huthwaite of Bristol. A watering can fitted
into a bracket on a five-foot-long (1·5-metre) bamboo pole and activated
by a string pull, it was designed to help short persons and ladies water
plants on upper shelves. Or the many forms of tobacco fumigators with
bellows which frequently backfired and kippered the gardener as well
as his infested vegetation. These were the inspired toys of the middle-
class 'Villa' gardeners alight with enthusiasm for their healthful and
beneficial pastime. Oblivious to fashion, the walled kitchen garden
went on satisfactorily enough with the aid of the 'old-fashioned and
vulgar implements'. Not without a certain pride, for Robert
Thompson's *Gardener's Assistant* informed its readers that the English
spade had long been justly considered the best in the world.

A good Victorian spade had a handle of ash with a D-shaped
end to grip. The edge of the blade was steel and the upper part
the best scrap iron. The London Treaded Spade had a narrow
iron plate on top of the blade which supported the digger's boot
as he pushed the blade into the soil. Such a spade hung in the
tool shed at Chilton. It had a sister, a digging fork, also D-
handled and with four prongs. Both had been passed over in
favour of their modern lightweight comrades. A woodworm
had come and gone from the right-hand side of the fork's handle

but, lifted off the wall, the worn wood inside the stirruped D-shape felt as smooth as silk.

It took diligent searching to find other old tools and appliances. Age had withered and condemned some to odd uses; a sharp-pronged manure fork was acting as a prop for the old vinery door. Of two watering engines, one was without a pump, the other, minus its galvanised barrel, stood with rusting iron ribs empty and spectral in a corner of the north border. Sharing the potting shed with a four-legged fruit and flower handbarrow was an extraordinarily heavy elm wheelbarrow with a wooden wheel. On a nail inside Harry's office hung a pouch bag. The leather was rock-hard with dust and disuse, inside it was a small clawhammer. This was the bag the fruit journeyman wore. He slung it round his neck to leave his hands free as, for painstaking hours, he nailed and tagged the walled fruit. Many thousands of nail holes pitted the garden walls. Testing and tapping, the fruitman discarded old nails and inserted new ones to secure boiled strips of linen which would hold the trees firmly in place against the walls.

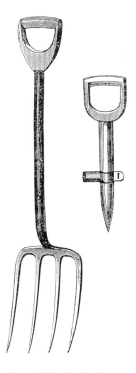

Above: Digging fork and dibber
Left: The nailbag and hammer go back into use
Below: Turfing iron (left) and garden line and reel

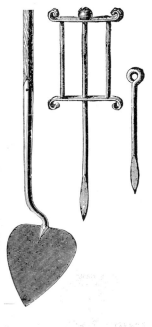

A rusting Patent American Tree Pruner with parrot-shaped blades was found lying across the rafters of the pot shed. Swan-necked draw hoes, old shovels, picks and dibbers were resting in various corners, while the heart-shaped turfing iron had already been brought back into use to slice the turves for our young fruit trees. A garden line with an iron reel turning on a spindle with a peg and a cord was found to help Alison align the borders. Harry also had an old watering can, not the tinned iron sort painted with red lead but a pretty ancient one, he thought, tucked away somewhere safe. In the same place, when he could search for it, was an old wooden rake. A pair of sulphur dusting bellows had existed, but just recently they had rotted away. There were still, however, small tin and wick tobacco fumigators in some of the glasshouses and two old brass water syringes, one working, one not.

Other finds were an iron double cylinder roller for the garden paths and, tucked up against the wall of Harry's cottage, a pair of cast-iron lantern cloches. They were rusty but most of the glass was still intact. One mysterious and ancient tool remained unidentified. It looked like

Clockwise from top left: Garden engine, watering pot, short-handled fork, garden roller, three thrust hoes and four draw hoes

a dock weeder without its curved iron fulcrum. It was obviously a candidate for museum experts. Rounded up, de-rusted, oiled and reassembled, these were to go back into service in the garden.

Hunt-the-tools had been fun. More serious work lay ahead. The soil at Chilton was a medium loam with chalk beneath. Thankfully, its lightness spared us the need to trench it. Trenching is mentioned in modern gardening manuals but it is doubtful whether many people still practise it and, if they do, whether with the dedication and to the depths carried out in days gone by.

Explained simply, it is a method of digging deeply, sometimes down to three spits – equivalent to the depth of three spade blades. The object is to provide fresh and deeper soil for plants by bringing the subsoil to the surface. This is piled in ridges and left for the frost to break down. Trenching was a useful job in winter months when the weather brought other work to a standstill. Gardeners were, however, advised against sending out their men with mattocks to break ground iron hard with frost. To have men throw top spits which were nothing but solid lumps into a trench was deemed to be a great waste of labour. Better by far to have men undercover making pegs and repairing appliances for shade and shelter in readiness for the busy summer months. Warnings were also issued against trenching thin soil too deeply. All the benefits of loosening and sweetening could be lost if an inexperienced man brought too much poor subsoil to the surface. In extreme cases, this could cause the ground to become barren and the whole patch would have to be retrenched to resurrect the topsoil. If there was any doubt as to the quality of subsoil it was considered wise to 'bastard' trench. By this method the first spit was removed and the soil of the second spit beneath it loosened with a fork. When the top spit was replaced the two soils would mingle. This was thought to improve considerably soils of unpromising structure and texture.

Although it was a more laborious process, the benefits of trenching could be further enhanced by a sort of manure sandwich, which involved introducing manure between the spits. This was supposed to encourage fine beans, peas, cauliflowers, broccoli and cabbages. Putting the manure at the bottom of the trench beneath the two spits was recommended for obtaining gigantic root vegetables such as parsnips, carrots and salsify.

It would be quite a relief to leave manures buried two spits under for it is all too easy, given the vast range and volume of application attributable to nineteenth-century manures, to become, well, rather bogged down. The types used could, given a lyrical turn of mind, compete well against the reading of the shipping forecast: lime, mild

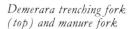

Demerara trenching fork (top) and manure fork

and caustic, marl, gypsum, sulphate of ammonia (a by-product of gasworks), salt, guano, bones, dried blood, horn, hoof, wool waste, fish guano, farmyard dung, compost, sewage, scutch (the waste from glue making), bristles, feathers, leather scrap, soot, seaweed, blubber, graves (tallow chandlers' refuse) and finally, although no doubt one or two might have been forgotten, liberal sprinklings of charcoal either for itself or to tone down the hum given off by organic manure heaps.

In an effort to disentangle the range and reasons for all the above you have to remember that a fertiliser is any substance which contains nitrogen, phosphoric acid or potash, the three essential ingredients which might be lacking in soil and which a plant needs to grow. In the nineteenth century the early soil chemists made two categories: direct manures and indirect manures.

Into the first category fell bone, blood, hoof, guano (more on this later) and superphosphates. Into the second category fell lime, salt, marl, etc. Sewage and farmyard dung conveniently fitted into both categories. Farmyard dung was probably the most prolifically used manure in the fruit and vegetable garden. A quote from Shirley Hibberd's *Profitable Gardening* graphically tables its value in ascending order:

> If a given quantity of land, sown without manure yields three times the seed employed, then the same quantity of land will produce five times the quantity sown when manured with old herbage, putrid grass or leaves, garden stuff, etc, seven times with cow-dung, nine times with pigeon-dung, ten times with horse-dung, twelve times with human urine, twelve times with goat-dung, twelve times with sheep-dung, and fourteen times with human manure, or bullocks' blood.

Horse-dung brought in from the stable yard was good for cold, stiff soil because it was 'hot'. The heat was attributable to the rich diet of artificial foods a horse eats and the fact it drank less water than a cow. The heat could become too much of a good thing as used unwisely fermented horse manure could damage plants. However, it did come into its own in another department of the garden as a provider of heat for forcing vegetables in winter. If you consider that one reasonably-fed horse produces 12,450 pounds (5647 kilograms) of droppings a year (which would make about 30 tons of farmyard manure) and then think about how many horses there were in Victorian times, the sheer magnitude of this source of manure becomes very obvious.

Cow-dung was as important as horse-dung. It was regarded as 'cool', due to the cows' more natural diet of grass and water. It was considered to be particularly good for fruit trees. Pig-dung was favoured for growing pineapples, but the most valuable dung of all was sheep-dung. This contains more nitrogen and phosphates than the other two.

The value of sheep-dung was not lost on a Mr Fleming of Trentham in Staffordshire. Mr Fleming constructed a loosely boarded wooden platform, placed a quantity of loam and turf beneath it, drove his sheep on to the platform and penned them there. The sheep-dung and urine dropped through the boards and percolated into the compost below. Once nicely saturated, Mr Fleming removed the mixture to his potting sheds.

E. S. Delamer warned in *The Kitchen Garden* against valuable manure sources being allowed to go away in the shape of perquisites claimed by servants.

Bones, for instance, are mostly sold by the cook or kitchen-maid; but wherever there is a garden, not a bone ought to be allowed to leave the premises. Bone dust, pounded bones, bones in almost any shape, are essential manures for turnips, asparagus and most other culinary plants. Not only are plants grown with their aid finer to the eye but, what is better, they are more nutritious to the human system.

Bones first started to be used as a manure in 1774. In 1829 a Mr Anderson of Dundee introduced machinery which would break them into half- and quarter-inch (1·2- and 0·6-cm) pieces and also produce bone dust. The use of bones gained in popularity to such an extent that the home supply ran out and great quantities were brought into Hull Docks from Germany and northern Europe. So large were these imports that the following grim statement was issued:

England is robbing all other countries of the condition of their fertility. Already, in her eagerness for bones, she has turned up the battlefields of Leipzig, of Waterloo, and of the Crimea; already from the catacombs of Sicily she has carried away the skeletons of many successive generations. Annually she removes from the shores of other countries to her own the manurial equivalent of three millions and half of men, whom she takes from us the means of supporting, and squanders down her sewers to the sea. Like a vampire, she hangs upon the neck of Europe – nay, of the entire world! – and sucks the heart-blood from nations without a thought of justice towards them, without a shadow of lasting advantage to herself.

The writer was Baron Liebig, who worked in Munich and was one of a group of men investigating the new science concerning the chemistry of soil. Early horticulturalists had believed that the value of manure came not from the nutrients it supplied to plants but from the fact that it broke down the soil into pieces small enough for plants to absorb whatever goodness was in the soil naturally. This emphasis on the value of well-tilled soil was the theory on which Jethro Tull based his horse-hoe system. In 1850, however, chemists A. Huxtable and T. Thompson poured liquid manure through soil and found that after the liquid had filtered through it lost its colour and smell. Subsequent experiments showed that soil 'fixed' and held constituents found in manure, releasing them in a gradual supply as and when the plants required them.

Baron Liebig believed that perfect agriculture was the true foundation of all trades and industry. Thus it was essential to have an understanding of the nutrition of vegetables and the influence of soils and actions of manures upon them. He was the first to estimate the importance of minerals as plant food, but his most interesting discovery takes us back to bones. In 1840 he added sulphuric acid to bones and discovered that the acid made the phosphate in the bones water-soluble and so more easily absorbed into the soil. The addition of acid doubled the efficiency of bones as manure. However, it fell to another man, John Bennet Lawes, to capitalise on this discovery.

Lawes was a gentleman farmer with a passionate interest in science. He converted a bedroom at his family home, Rothamsted Manor, near Harpenden in Hertfordshire, into a laboratory. This greatly annoyed his mother as it was one of the best bedrooms. He followed this by turning an old barn near the house into a chemical factory and tried new ways of making chlorine gas with sulphuric acid, but without success. A friend who was a manufacturer asked Lawes if he could find a use for all the bone charcoal which was a by-product from his factory. At the time, bonemeal was being used by farmers and gardeners as a fertiliser but it seemed to work only on soil in certain areas of the country and Rothamsted was not one of these. Lawes, no doubt aware of Liebig's experiments, came to the conclusion that bonemeal was effective only in acid soil because the acid content caused a chemical reaction, making the bonemeal release phosphate. If the soil was alkaline the phosphate remained locked in and the bonemeal was a poor fertiliser.

Sir John Bennet Lawes

Taking some charred bones from his friend's factory, Lawes added to them some of the sulphuric acid which remained from his unsuccessful gas experiments. By mixing the two together he hoped the acid would make the phosphate in the charred bones water-soluble and so, when it rained, more available to plants. He tried out the new mixture on plants in pots and on turnips in a field and, whereas before Rothamsted soil had not received any benefit from bonemeal, now the results were quite spectacular.

Lawes quickly patented his method and all other ways of treating phosphates with acid so that they could be used as fertilisers. In 1842 he opened a factory at Deptford for manufacturing his new product which he called 'Super Phosphate of Lime'. There was considerable family opposition – it was not then considered proper for a gentleman to deal in trade, particularly a trade which involved using old bones as manure. His wife and family were convinced he would be ruined. They were wrong. The business prospered and in July of the following year, 1843, he placed his first advertisement in the *Gardeners' Chronicle*:

J. B. LAWES'S PATENT MANURES, composed of Super Phosphate of Lime, Phosphate of Ammonia, Silicate of Potass, etc, are now for sale at his factory, Deptford-creek, London, price 4s 6d per bushel. These substances can be had separately; the Super Phosphate of Lime alone is recommended for fixing the Ammonia of Dung-heaps, Cesspools, Gas Liquor, &c.
Price 4s 6d per bushel.

Later that year Lawes had another success. The famous botanist and geologist, John Stevens Henslow, was staying with his family at Felixstowe and he noticed that one of the layers making up the cliff face contained a bed of rolled brown pebbles. The pebbles had once formed an ancient beach and when Henslow examined them he found that they often contained a shark's tooth or other organic remains. This made him suspect that the pebbles had phosphate of lime in them. He contacted Lawes who asked for a ton of the nodules to be sent to him. Lawes experimented with them and the result was a new and successful fertiliser called 'coprolite'. Several landowners who were lucky enough to have deposits of the nodules on their land cashed in on the find and became very rich.

Seeing the success of Lawes' business, other companies began to trade on his idea and Lawes had to go through several court cases to defend his patent. One particular offender was the London Manure Company. In 1851 Lawes finally made them agree to his terms: they could use bones to make their superphosphate but if they used minerals, such as the phosphate of lime nodules, they had to pay him royalties of ten shillings (50p) for every ton of phosphate used. Another firm, Fisons of Thetford, who had been riding on the phosphate bandwagon, also agreed to the same terms. It did not, however, end there. When greater quantities of mineral phosphate were discovered in other parts of the country, rival firms tried to make Lawes lift his restrictions. There was yet another court case with eminent scientists giving evidence and judgment was passed that owing to the time and money that Lawes had spent on perfecting mineral phosphate as a fertiliser, his monopoly could continue. In 1882 Lawes sold his company for the considerable sum of £300,000.

An interesting tailpiece is that Lawes' experimental work still goes on today. In addition to running his manure business he had joined forces with an eminent chemist, Doctor Joseph Henry Gilbert, and together they carried on scientific experiments at Rothamsted. One of their experiments was to divide a field, called Broadbalk, into strips. On each strip they grew wheat with a different fertiliser. On one strip, farmyard manure, on another chemical manure, on a third no manure at all. Each year they did exactly the same, making detailed recordings of the crop yield from each strip. Today Rothamsted is a government horticultural and agricultural research station and the same Broadbalk experiment is continued. It is an invaluable asset for scientists to have detailed records of one area of land spanning such a long period and it is remarkable that one particular piece of ground which is growing wheat has had no manure, artificial or otherwise, on it since 1843.

The results of the Broadbalk experiment are stored at Rothamsted in a building the size of a small warehouse. It is an extraordinary place filled with close-standing rows of shelves, towering up twenty to thirty feet (6 to 9 metres). Each shelf is filled with row upon row of glass bottles. Anyone working in the store is given a construction worker's hard hat in case any of the ancient bottles come tumbling down. Some bottles are filled with soil, others with grain. The older bottles are sealed with lead and labelled in faded brown ink. The newer samples are in metal containers. The close proximity and tremendous height of the shelving makes the place dark and awesome. It is a most odd feeling to walk through the dim narrow alleyways flanked by cliff-high bottles.

The trials and tribulations of our attempts to track down a bag of guano for Chilton might deter less determined garden restorers. Guano was the wonder manure, without which no Victorian garden would have been complete. Lord Derby first brought guano into Liverpool Docks in 1840. From 1840 until the end of the nineteenth century, 5 million tons were brought into this country from Peru alone. Checking with the Department of Trade it appears that an infinitesimal 2000 tons are imported today, but where it goes to remains a trade secret. We would have to rely on farmyard manure for Chilton, but the great guano story is worth telling.

Guano is a corruption of the Quechua dialect word 'huanu' meaning dung. It is the centuries-old deposits of dried excrement from seabirds and sea creatures such as seals and walruses. Deposits sometimes a hundred feet (30 metres) thick were found on the coastlines of Peru and Chile. The best quality came from three small islands off the coast of Peru known as the Chincha Islands. Here, with little rain to wash away its nutritional value, the guano was rich in nitrogen and phosphates.

Guano overshadowed farmyard manure and bones and paved the way for artificial manuring. Two ounces per yard (60 grams per metre) sprinkled over onions made the onions grow to twice the size of untreated ones. An ounce and a half (42 grams) spread over potatoes quickly brought luxuriant growth. Such power did have its drawbacks.

Patches of young seedling strawberries were prone to curl up and die under the strength of guano and a correspondent writing to the *Cottage Gardener* in October 1852 tells how nine-parts earth and one-part guano half destroyed his newly-planted Brussels sprouts. A safe liquid mixture was thought to be half an ounce (14 grams) to a gallon (4·5 litres) of water. This recipe apparently never failed to be 'productive of vigour'.

The power of guano as a manure had been recognised by the Incas who imposed a penalty of death on anyone disturbing the seabirds on the deposits. In 1669 the Earl of Sandwich translated a passage written by a Spanish priest thirty years earlier. The passage describes the power of guano to make ploughed ground fertile and ends by saying:

The quantities and virtues of this and of many other samples of the New World are a large field for ingenious persons to discourse philosophically upon, when they shall bend their minds more to the searching out of truth than riches.

Riches, rather than truth, were unfortunately the main aim of the day some 200 years later. A substance so eagerly sought by gardeners was easy game for the unscrupulous. Guano was brown and powdery with a pungent smell. If it looked right and smelt right, people bought it. High prices were often asked and obtained for substances that owed their bulk more to sawdust, ricemeal, peat, chalk or ashes of various kinds rather than pure guano. The wary could carry out a test to ascertain whether their guano had been adulterated. True guano ash was whitish-grey. If a small sample of guano was burnt and produced red ash this indicated that a mineral substance containing iron had been added. Very white ash indicated the addition of salt or chalk.

In the early 1850s 'considerable unease' was voiced in Britain that so much guano being imported, not only by the British but by other nations, would cause the supplies to run out. Admiral Moresby, the British Commander in the Pacific, was dispatched to ascertain how much was left. He reported back the fairly alarming news that supplies of worthwhile guano from the Chincha Islands would be exhausted in eight or nine years. Other sites were sought, and guano was found in North America, the West Indies, Australia, Asia, Africa and the Pacific Islands. In 1897 the Chemical Union of Ipswich was even offering Canary guano   not from the bird but from the islands. At the turn of the century guano lost its popularity to two artificial nitrogenous manures – sodium nitrate, mined from the nitrate-fields of South America, and sulphate of ammonia, a by-product of gasworks and from shaleworks in Scotland.

CHAPTER SIX

•

Planning and arranging vegetables – Attaining the 'highest style of cultivation' – Seakale and the vegetable fruit-stalk. Some vegetable oddities explained.

SNOW had fallen. From wall to wall and from the glasshouses downwards it blotted the garden at Chilton into a flat, bare glare. A flatness broken only by the rounded white mountain range which marked the run, east to west, of submerged coldframes. A few brave sprigs of box edging, taller than their companions, stood dark green against the white, marking like isolated sentinels the lost paths below.

It was on this bitterly cold day that we met in Harry's cottage and spread his table with catalogues, old manuals and empty notebooks. Now was the time to plan the layout of vegetables in the garden and the varieties to be planted.

When a gardener enters upon his first responsible situation he should make it one of his first duties to take stock of the kitchen garden and, having ascertained as soon as possible the requirements, likes, and dislikes of the family, he should arrange his crops for the following season.

Snow gave little opportunity for outside work

We had no 'family' to supply and so this advice given in the *Journal of Horticulture* for 1877, although noted, couldn't be acted upon. However, our intention from the outset of the project had been to reconstruct a working nineteenth-century fruit and vegetable garden, and to this end we intended following as closely as possible a traditional layout of crops. The crops were to be nineteenth-century varieties, if obtainable.

First of all we thought about the borders surrounding the insides of the four walls. The walls had the young fruit planted against them. Care had obviously to be taken. Dark warnings against the destructive effects of cropping fruit borders with vegetables were given in a number of the old manuals. No labourer's spade should come within six feet (2 metres) of the wall if the fruit trees were expected to flourish, said one. The *Gardener* for 1869 swept into turbulent prose in an effort to safeguard the roots of fruit trees:

> Cast down, torn up, cut asunder, they are not destroyed. In the silence, in the darkness, exposed to freezing cold, benumbed with chilling water, they work bravely on to recover their misfortune, resolving to live, and not to die. But the warfare with our cruel culture is unequal. Once a year, sometimes much oftener, we attack them with our spades. Hardly have they had time to gather up their energies and heal their wounds, than they are made to bleed afresh.

To cause our carefully-chosen and sometimes rare fruit trees such agonies was obviously to be avoided!

We knew however that to make walled gardens as productive as possible the fruit borders were cropped with smaller kinds of vegetables that did not root deeply. The fruit borders, particularly the warm, south-facing one beneath the north wall, were invaluable. The south-facing border at Chilton was far wider than the other three fruit borders. This was traditional and sensible for here the border would have been divided into sections and the warmth gained by its position used to bring on early peas, potatoes, carrots, turnips, cauliflowers and beans. The warmth needed to grow early salad crops such as lettuce and radishes could be obtained by placing the seedlings under a series of glass cloches or handlights in the south border. Towards the end of the year the same warm position could be used to bring on French beans, spinach and turnips, as well as salading.

The borders beneath the west and east walls were planted with small crops which did not need large squares of ground. They provided seedbeds for cabbages, lettuce and temporary pricking out of celery. They were also useful for currants and gooseberries which, partially shaded, would produce their fruit late enough to be used for autumnal desserts. Cut flowers and herbs were also traditionally planted in either the west or east borders.

Curled solid white celery

Even the cold north-facing border at the bottom of the garden had its uses. It was a shady place for striking cuttings and for 'retarding' salad crops. It also provided a home for Alpine strawberries, late strawberries and raspberries.

In all, the crops raised on the fruit borders played an important part in helping to keep up the continuous, year-long supply of vegetables and salads to the house.

Continual supply was also the emphasis on the crops produced in the large central plots of the garden. This was used for the important crops: cabbages, cauliflowers, potatoes and beans. Tall crops such as peas, beans, raspberries, gooseberries, currants and Jerusalem artichokes were generally planted in a line from north to south instead of east to west. This gave them an equal share of sunshine, overcame the problem of their shading vegetables grown behind and avoided damage by strong south-west winds. Open, sunny spots were planted out with strawberries and red and white currants.

A well-run kitchen garden would have had crops running in lines parallel with and at right angles to the main walls. Every variety would have been carefully labelled and placed where it could be read from the walks and the whole garden would have been kept in what was called 'the highest style of cultivation'.

Climbing kidney bean

This highest style of cultivation would have included two important components, rotation and continuity. Rotation was the practice of moving the site of a crop so that it never grew in the same place in the next season. Crops grown in the same spot could cause a build-up of pests and disease and were also supposed to exhaust the soil. The early nineteenth-century chemist Sir Humphry Davy emphasised his view that each sort of plant drew nourishment from the ground peculiar to itself and, after a piece of ground had nourished one crop, another of a different description should succeed it.

This applied not only to varieties of vegetable but also to all the vegetables which fell into a particular category or classification. It was obvious that it was bad practice to have a crop of cabbages following on from cabbages, but it was just as bad to have the cabbages succeeded by Brussels sprouts, broccoli, savoy or any other member of the brassica classification. Similarly, carrots, beet, parsnips and salsify were all regarded as one family.

One method of rotation was to have brassicas, which were known to be greedy feeders, easily exhausting the soil, grown on manured ground which had rested, perhaps having supported a strawberry bed for some time. The brassicas, known as 'deterioraters', could then be followed by root crops such as potatoes, carrots, onions and beet,

Savoy cabbage (left) and cauliflower

known as 'preparers'. These in turn could be followed by 'surface' crops such as French beans, peas and salads before starting the entire cycle again.

'The continuous supply of good vegetables, including salads is often the most difficult as well as the most important part of the gardener's duties. Much skill and attention are required to have cabbages early in April; peas from May to November; lettuces, broccoli or cauliflower always.' Thus the *Journal of Horticulture* advised and, in the same year, 1877, horticultural journalist Shirley Hibberd made an even plainer statement: 'In a private establishment it is a mark of good management if the gardener can cut broccoli or cauliflower any day of the year.'

Achieving continuous supplies was the second part of keeping the garden in 'the highest style of cultivation'. Whatever the climatic difficulties, the head gardener was expected always to provide sufficient diversity and quantity of vegetables to meet all occasions. This could be achieved by a variety of methods. Planting on a 'hotbed' of manure, or in the warm south border, or 'retarding' in the cooler north border were all practised. But before plants could be nurtured, 'forced' or 'retarded' they had to be sown. The backbone of continuous supply depended on the times of sowing.

Successional sowing necessitated the gardener thinking ahead. To keep up a succession of cauliflowers, three or four sowings had to be made: the first, on a slight hotbed of manure, in February or very early March; the second and larger sowing about the second of April on to open ground; and the last sowing in the middle of August, these to stand through the winter. Any plants sown later in the autumn could be pricked out under frames to protect them from severe weather. Broccolis also had to have three or four sowings each season and at least a dozen varieties were sown. Walcheren broccoli, introduced in 1844, was the greatest standby. It could be sown at almost any season and cut at almost any season. Mr Hibberd believed that a master of broccoli culture could, by good management, cut beautiful white heads of medium size very nearly all the year round and if need be the whole circle of the year could be compassed with it. Cabbages filled in any gaps left by cauliflowers or broccoli or took the place of any crop that had failed. It was good practice to sow a pinch every month of the year, raising the young plants in frames from November to January.

In addition to the hardy vegetables, the succession of 'forced' winter vegetables such as seakale, asparagus, rhubarb and mushrooms had to be kept up. There was, however, a trap to catch even the most conscientious and far-thinking head gardener. A bitter entry in the *Journal of Horticulture* for March 1878 records it: 'We have often had fine crops to supply the wants of a company expected, but when the company came three weeks after the time specified, the cream of the crops was over.'

Another complaint was that head gardeners were not always given prior notice that company was to arrive and were expected to produce delicacies at a day's notice. It was particularly hurtful that the house-keeper, the steward and the cook were forewarned but that the head gardener had to glean such information where he could. 'A man really worth anything will be too independent for such underhand knowledge' was the general opinion amongst head gardeners.

Peas and beans were regarded as the most important of all the kitchen garden crops. Great prestige was attached to producing early crops, particularly peas. Head gardeners vied with one another to be first.

The fourth of June, King George III's birthday, had always been the target date but by careful 'forwarding' and protecting a crop of green peas could be sent up to the house even earlier. Mr D. Bain, gardener to Waresley Park Gardens at St Neots, wrote to the seeds firm Sutton and Sons in 1865 to say that he had gathered a dish of their Ringleader peas on the twenty-fourth of May. Mr Bain's letter was usefully integrated by Suttons into their 1866 catalogue, along with extracts of letters from twenty other satisfied customers each extolling the virtues of Ringleader.

This double spread of quotes prefaces five sections of pea seeds, each section containing six or more varieties. The First Division for the

Ringleader pea

earliest crop was for sowing from November to January and the resultant peas gathered in May and June. The Second Division was to be sown from January to February and gathered in June. The Third Division was to be sown from February to March and gathered in June and early July. The Fourth Division was to be sown in March and gathered in July. The Fifth Division, for the latest crops, was to be sown in April and May and gathered in July, August and September. From this it can be seen that garden peas could be sent to the house from May until September.

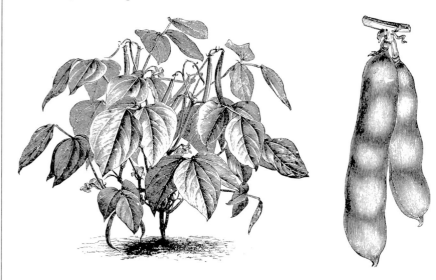

Far left: Dwarf French bean
Left: Broad bean
Right (from top): French bell jar, English bell jar and lantern cloche

All this proved daunting reading as we sat around Harry's sitting-room table. Harry alleviated some of the despondency by admitting that in the past he had always managed to provide a dish of peas on Cheltenham Gold Cup Day which was in mid-March. Suitably encouraged, we began to make a list of the vegetables which would have been grown in a Victorian walled garden.

The list went well until we got to 'Garlick'. Although this was noted in several of the old books, Brian Halliwell, Assistant Curator from the Royal Gardens at Kew, who had come down to advise at our meeting, thought that garlic might not have been grown, particularly during the first part of the nineteenth century, owing to the anti-French feeling at the time. We loyally struck garlic off the list. Another question mark was raised over pumpkins. These were variously mentioned as 'pompions' or 'gourds'. Brian felt that a serious working kitchen garden would not have bothered with them, considering their value to be more ornamental than culinary. Although we intended to be fairly serious, the thought of not having 'their luxuriant vines; their bold foliage;

and their noble-looking fruit' was slightly distressing. Eventually, pumpkins were left on the list, particularly as Harry felt they would grow well in one of the coldframes.

With the list made, the next task was to select a suitable place for each vegetable on a large hand-drawn map of the garden. We started with the extreme left-hand corner of the warm, south-facing border. By the gate which led out to Harry's cottage, we put a clump of sweet fennel, useful for its culinary aromatic leaves. Next we drew a series of small circles to indicate glass bell jars and a series of crossed squares to indicate lantern cloches, which would give protection to winter lettuce, early carrots, radishes and Lamb's lettuce. The glass bell jars were rather special antiques from a hoard found some years ago at Evesham in Worcestershire. One example is now in Evesham Museum and we were lucky enough to be loaned ours from someone living locally. The glass knob on each jar had long ago been broken off to prevent it catching the sun and acting like a magnifying glass to burn the crop inside. The lantern cloches were the ones we had rescued from Harry's cottage garden, where they'd been put 'safely' some time ago with the idea that one day they might be done up. Their day had come. Alison was marked down to wirebrush the rust off the metal parts, undercoat and topcoat them white and wash the glass panes. Very attractive they would look against the old pink brick of the south wall.

The crop plan for the south border continued with two rows of short peas and a few rows of kohlrabi, both the white and the more attractive purple Vienna variety. Looking like a swollen radish growing above ground, kohlrabi was an import from German gardens. It found popularity amongst Victorians who favoured a 'strong cabbagy taste'. The swollen stem was capable of growing to the size of an orange but once it got past the size of a hen's egg many gardeners considered kohlrabi too coarse to send up for the dining-table. It could, of course, continue to be eaten in the servants' hall.

Besides the kohlrabi, spaces were marked for spinach and radishes. Places were then allocated for vegetables which could be blanched for winter salad. Blanching whitens and sweetens. It is achieved by blocking the light from a plant, either by covering it with a pot, piling earth or straw round it or tying up its leaves. Endive was a popular vegetable for blanching. Broad-leaved endive looks like a cross between lettuce and cabbage and, grown in succession, it would keep a place in the produce basket all through the year. It was the practice in the autumn to tie up a few plants each week with bast or raffia in order to keep up the supply. In frosty weather the plants were protected by straw mats or dug up and placed upright in a cellar with earth still hanging from their roots. In the English edition of Mme Vilmorin-Andrieux's *The Vegetable Garden*, published in 1885, endive is described as 'most highly esteemed for table use'. As well as having a crop in the south border we could bring successional crops on in the coldframes.

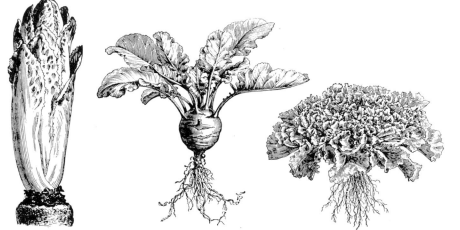

Left to right: Witloof chicory, kohlrabi, broadleafed endive, skirret

The other popular blanching vegetable was chicory. Witloof or Brussels chicory, when covered with soil, produces a head like a whitened Cos lettuce. As for Cos lettuce itself and particularly the early Bath Brown variety, this was listed to go under some of Harry's lantern cloches at the end of the south border. The cloches would also provide shelter for small crops of Lamb's lettuce and maybe a few early potatoes and beetroot. Fronting the cloches could be a row of dandelions, the leaves of which are also useful for winter salads. We read that 127 years earlier, E. S. Delamer in his book *The Kitchen Garden* noted that in France dandelion shoots were blanched by the earth of molehills. Garden boys were sent to collect this beautifully friable soil which was trickled around the plants to be blanched.

The west wall border was plotted next. We started at the top end with the curious old vegetable skirret. Skirret had the advantage of being both useful and ornamental. Its roots are tender and sweet for boiling and its three- to four-foot-high (1-metre) leaves with small white flowers make an attractive addition to what would be the beginning of a stretch of herbs. We were following tradition by putting the herbs in a border easily accessible from the pathway. The herbs were the most-used culinary ones: parsley, mint, sage, thyme, horse-radish, fennel, marjoram, bay and tarragon.

In amongst the herbs, spots were marked for various small kinds of onions. First, shallots for pickling, then the Egyptian or tree onion, reputedly introduced into England from Canada in 1820 where it had been popular amongst the lumbermen of Maine for flavouring their broth. Harry knew this onion as 'the upside-down one' which seemed as good a description as any, for its bulbs grow not in the ground but at the top of its stalk. Being the size of marbles they would also be useful for pickling. The Welsh onion, or ciboule, also had a special use: it forms a tapering root instead of bulbs and head gardeners planted it as an insurance, in case cold weather killed off the early spring onions.

Next in line came a neglected and forgotten vegetable – the spinach-like Good King Henry. Its decline outside the walled garden probably came about with the popularity of cultivated spinach. Spinach has the advantage over Good King Henry in that its leaves will stay fresh far longer after cutting. Good King Henry did, however, have its own attributes. The first leaves could be used in salad, the older leaves served like spinach while the shoots of the plant, when as thick as the little finger, could be boiled and eaten like asparagus. All valuable assets to a head gardener constantly looking for continuity and variety.

If our reconstruction project was to be a success continuity and variety were two essentials. As well as being productive, the garden had to be attractive. Wasn't it, after all, often displayed proudly to his friends by the master of the house?

The prettiest of all the vegetables on our list was the purple and white variegated kale. The kale could be cooked like ordinary cabbage, particularly after a frost, and its raw leaves were useful garnishing for winter salads. In some gardens it was grown as edging to the vegetable borders. If not grown as edging, most gardeners grew a row or two somewhere, for they were conversation pieces, particularly welcome at times such as Sunday morning when the whole family toured the garden on their way back from church. It was decided that ornamental kale would give colour to the west border, places were also reserved for it in one or two of the coldframes which ran across the top of the main vegetable plots. A patch of orach, a native of Tartary according to Mme Vilmorin-Andrieux, and useful for mixing with spinach to modify its acidity, was to separate the ornamental kale from its very different but equally interesting kin – seakale.

Recently an article in a popular glossy magazine under the title 'Forgotten Vegetables' featured seakale. Reading Victorian horticultural manuals it is surprising that seakale ever passed from culinary knowledge. How could one forget a delicacy that rich people strove to have ready to cut at Christmas, that was served 'on sippets of toasted bread drenched in white sauce or melted butter' and described as 'a beautiful branch carved in ivory'? The first seakale was recorded as

Seakale

seen in Chichester market by a Mr William Jones of Chelsea. This was wild seakale gathered locally from the seashore. The vegetable was introduced to London markets by a Mr Curtis who in 1799 wrote 'Directions for Cultivating the Crambe Maritima or Seakale'.

In gardens seakale plants were grown from seed or cuttings from roots. During the summer months the peculiar silvery-grey foliage of the kale flourished, but it was when the first frosts shrivelled the leaves that the work of producing the vegetable as a delicacy began. According to *The Kitchen Garden*, six or seven weeks before the plants were wanted for cutting, they were covered with pots and the pots in turn covered with fresh, long, stable manure just ready to begin fermenting. The temperature of the manure was tested by thrusting a stick into it and feeling the heat of the stick when it was withdrawn. By this method blanched shoots were 'forced' from the seakale crowns beneath the pots. Plants could also be taken up and forced on hotbeds of manure or put into hothouses. It certainly seemed worth brushing the soil of ages off a vegetable which gave the 'happy combination of the flavours of asparagus and cauliflower', particularly as the shadiness of the lower stretch of the west border seemed ideal for it. We decided to order fifty crowns of seakale from one of the few firms that still grow them.

Following the garden plan downwards led from the intended seakale plantation at the end of the west border to the beginnings of the cold, north-facing border which stretched along the bottom of the garden. The first part of the north border seemed suitable for the useful and decorative Swiss chard, both red and white varieties, which could be boiled like spinach. The chard should crop all through the summer and autumn. Alongside the chard, maybe some leeks, then a few rows of ornamental kale followed by a space for late salading and finally, in the cold end-corner where the frost always seemed to hang the longest, some hardy cottager's kale.

Continuing upwards from the end of the north border to the east-facing one, planning became relatively easy. Most of this border could be given over to growing cut flowers. These would have been useful to the head gardener who could use them to supply the house without having to deplete the flowers in the pleasure grounds. Four wigwam shapes were also drawn at intervals down the east border; two to be trained with sweet peas and two for scarlet runner beans.

Moving into the centre of the garden, more flowers were planned to fill two six-foot-wide (2-metre) borders, one on either side of the central walkway which ran north to south down through the main vegetable plots. Flowers in a vegetable garden might seem odd but the central walkway was an important focal point of most walled gardens. This

1 (right) A vestige of the Victorian traditions which once linked garden and dining room still exists at Chatsworth House in Derbyshire. Head gardener Dennis Hopkins and butler Henry Coleman first set and then carefully check the positioning of fruit and flowers on the dining table

I

2

3

4

5

6

2, 3 and 4 My first sight of the unrestored walled kitchen garden at Chilton

5 The head gardener's house, built close to the walled garden and overlooking the River Kennet

6 Almost two years after my first visit – the garden in late summer, fully restored

7 and 8 A flurry of cherry blossom on a fan-trained Early Rivers

9 Pear blossom later gave way to young fruit setting on the trained trees

7

8

9

10

10 *The pot shed where the crock boy spent long hours pot washing*

11 *Harry preparing for the summer: cuttings from 'bedding-out' plants like geraniums were potted up and overwintered in the glasshouses of the kitchen garden*

12 *Late autumn sunlight helped dry a varied harvest of seeds and flowers*

13 *Old tools scattered around glasshouses and tucked into forgotten corners were rounded up, cleaned and hung, ready for use*

11

12

14

15

16

17

18

19

14 *Summer seakale foliage and the Victorian beehive in a sheltered corner of the garden*

15 *A lantern handlight, one of several which helped to bring on early salading in the south-facing border*

16 *Ripening figs*

17 *Packing figs with leaves and tissue paper was an art Harry had learned from his uncle, head gardener to the Earl of Selborne*

18 *White Dutch currants – a popular dessert*

19 *The more acid red currants were thought best suited to preserves and wine making*

20 *Peaches grown against the garden's warm south-facing wall*

was the pathway down which visitors were most likely to stroll, so the more attractive it could be made, the better. It was also a useful place for growing the beloved Victorian *immortelles*, the flowers which could be dried for winter decoration.

Lily of the valley

In addition to flowers to enhance the sides of the central walkway, we had to think of climbing shrubs for the hooped iron arches at the beginning and end of the walk. Against the span of hoops which ran over the centre of the walk we had already planted young cordon-trained apples and pears, with a view to these eventually forming a blossom and fruit archway. A suggested list of possible plants for the end arches included golden hop, clematis and roses for the first arch and on the end one down at the bottom by the north border, clematis mixed with winter jasmine. Two more flowers were considered before we returned to planning vegetables: fragrant violets and lily of the valley, both of which could be brought on in coldframes and which would have been specially sent up for the lady of the house. The thought pleased Harry. Before the days of Chilton's decline he had always kept a few coldframes filled with early Parma violets. Courting garden apprentices had also been known to help themselves to a few. More mundane, but equally sought after, out-of-season crops could also come from the coldframes. Helped on by hotbeds made from fermenting manure, they could be the raising places for young carrots and potatoes and, once these were cleared, house peppers, ridge cucumbers, early beetroot and other crops which would respond to a little nurturing. For this Harry had a bed of soil which he reckoned was so rich he valued it at a guinea an ounce.

To anyone standing down by the north-facing wall and looking up at the garden in its unkempt state, one of the most prominent features would be a particularly scrubby rectangle of ground to the left of the row of coldframes. Cleared of its nettles and docks and treated to a wholesome amount of manure, this rectangle was intended to be the site for a late nineteenth-century favourite – rhubarb. Rhubarb was prized not only for its taste but for more personal reasons. A contributor to the *Cottage Gardener* in 1852, writing of a variety called Turkey rhubarb, found it to be 'most efficacious, both as an aperient and tonic medicine, in the latter case, in combination with ipecacuanha and Castile soap'. Perhaps its popularity at Christmas had as much to do with its purgative powers as its appearance as a forced winter delicacy.

A hundred or more varieties were bred during the Victorian era, although initially it had been thought of as an intrusion into British kitchen gardens. The Chinese species of rhubarb was first grown here successfully in the 1760s from seeds sent to the Botanical Gardens in

21 *The 'show' or stove house restored. This was the glasshouse in the kitchen garden that might be walked round and admired by the master of the house and his family after church on Sunday mornings (although always kept immaculate, the floor was washed and brushed minutes before the family arrived)*

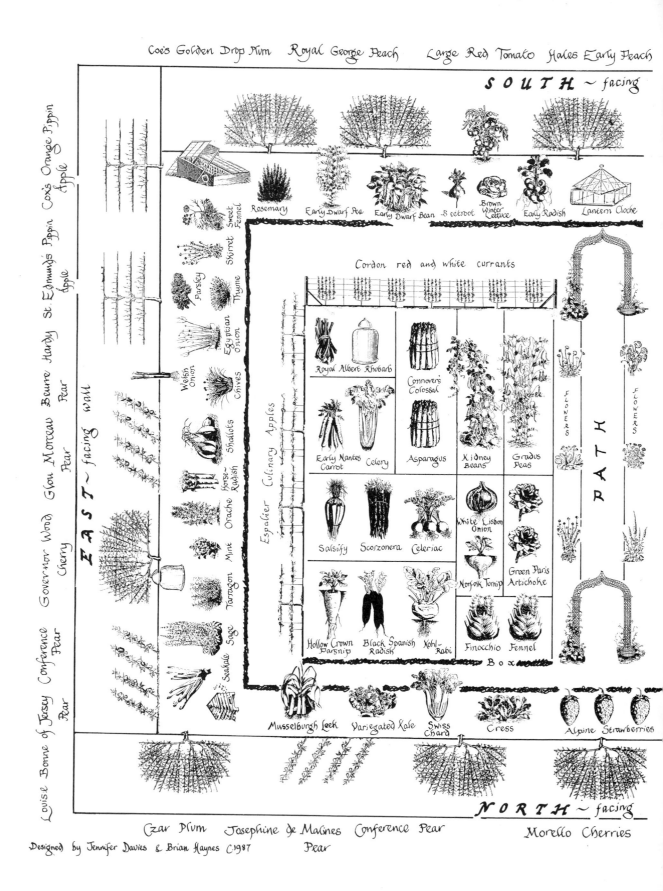

Coe's Golden Drop Plum   Royal George Peach   Large Red Tomato   Hales Early Peach

SOUTH ~ facing

Cox's Orange Pippin Apple

St Edmund's Pippin Apple

Beurre Hardy Pear

Glou Morceau Pear

Governor Wood Cherry

EAST ~ facing wall

Conference Pear

Louise Bonne of Jersey Pear

Rosemary

Sweet Fennel

Skirret

Parsley

Thyme

Egyptian Onion

Welsh Onion

Chives

Shallots

Horse Radish

Orache

Mint

Tarragon

Sage

Seakale

Early Dwarf Pea   Early Dwarf Bean   Beetroot   Brown Winter Lettuce   Early Radish   Lantern Cloche

Cordon red and white currants

Espalier Culinary Apples

Royal Albert Rhubarb   Connover's Colossal

Early Nantes Carrot   Celery   Asparagus   Kidney Beans   Gradus Peas

Salsify   Scorzonera   Celeriac   White Lisbon Onion   Green Paris Artichoke

Norfolk Turnip

Hollow Crown Parsnip   Black Spanish Radish   Kohl-Rabi   Finocchio Fennel

Box

Musselburgh Leek   Variegated Kale   Swiss Chard   Cress   Alpine Strawberries

FLOWERS   FLOWERS

PATH

NORTH ~ facing

Czar Plum   Josephine de Malines Pear   Conference Pear   Morello Cherries

Designed by Jennifer Davies & Brian Haynes ©1987

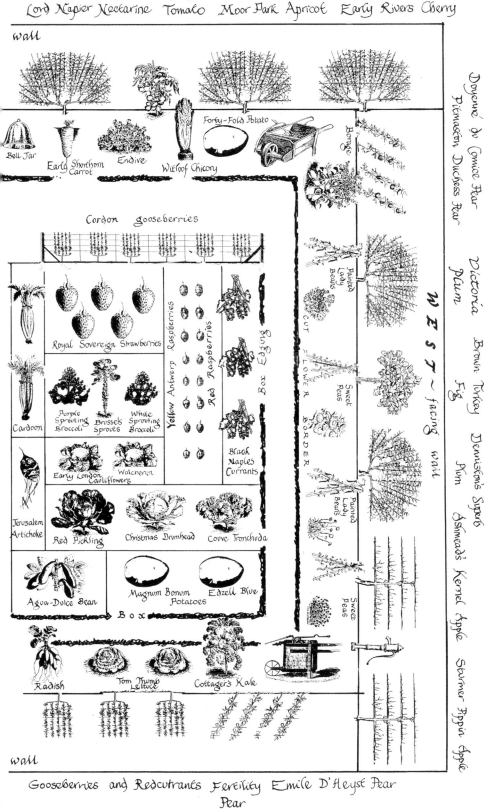

Lord Napier Nectarine   Tomato   Moor Park Apricot   Early Rivers Cherry

wall

Bell Jar

Early Shorthorn Carrot

Endive

Witloof Chicory

Forty-Fold Potato

Borage

Doyenné du Comice Pear

Pitmaston Duchess Pear

Victoria Plum

Brown Turkey Fig

Denniston's Superb Plum

Ashmead's Kernel Apple

Sturmer Pippin Apple

Cordon gooseberries

Royal Sovereign Strawberries

Yellow Antwerp Raspberries

Red Raspberries

Box Edging

Cardoon

Purple Sprouting Broccoli

Brussels Sprouts

White Sprouting Broccoli

Early London Cauliflowers

Walcheren

Black Naples Currants

Jerusalem Artichoke

Red Pickling

Christmas Drumhead

Couve Tronchuda

Agua-Dulce Bean

Magnum Bonum Potatoes

Edzell Blue

Box

CUT FLOWER BORDER

Planted Lady Beans

Sweet Peas

Planted Lady Beans

Sweet Peas

W E S T ~ facing wall

Radish

Tom Thumb Lettuce

Cottager's Kale

wall

Gooseberries and Redcurrants   Fertility Pear   Emile D'Heyst Pear

This is how the garden was eventually planted up – keeping roughly to the original plan except when it was found that in practice some vegetables fitted better elsewhere. For example, tall peas and beans were planted in the left-hand plot instead of the right, where their height acted as a windbreak to protect the fragile showy flowers beside the central path

Edinburgh by an English physician to the Russian Court. It did not, however, gain widespread cultivation until 1824, when a Scottish gardener, Jas Smith, began to force it in the same way as seakale was being forced. By covering a few crowns at a time with pots covered with fermented material or lifting the roots and putting them into heated houses with a covering of hay or fern to effect blanching, rhubarb could be supplied to the kitchen from December until spring. From the kitchen, the 'vegetable fruit-stalk' emerged transmuted into 'delicious and wholesome tarts and puddings' bound for the dining-table.

It seemed a pity at this juncture of our planning that no ample Victorian cook would conveniently reincarnate, complete with pine table, polished range and a posse of kitchen maids. But it could not be, and attention turned to looking at the plots of land on either side of the central walkway.

The two plots forming the bulk of the garden would originally have been given over to soft fruits and the main vegetable crops. At the top of the garden a pathway running west to east separated these plots from the horizontal run of coldframes. A small lavender hedge was planned to run along the tops of both borders, breaking in the middle where the first archway spanned the central walkway. In the upper part of the plots, directly behind the lavender edging, lines were drawn to represent rows of red and white currants and gooseberries. A fairly large area which caught the sun high up on the right-hand plot was designated for the main strawberry bed. From north to south down the far side of this plot would be rows of yellow and red raspberries and blackcurrants.

Below the soft fruits in each plot, sufficient room was allowed for one or two rows of main crop vegetables. In the two plots, we would put winter and spring cabbage including the old *Couve Tronchuda* or Portugal cabbage, which was introduced into Great Britain in 1821, kale, cauliflower and celery. Then the winter root vegetables: carrots, turnips, beetroot and two rare vegetables, salsify and scorzonera. These two vegetables were encouraged in Victorian gardens to give variety to the winter crops. Salsify was sometimes called 'goat's beard' owing to the shape of its leaves. It was also known as 'vegetable oyster' because of its oyster like flavour when the roots were boiled and served with white sauce. Scorzonera is named for what it is – *scorza* meaning root and *nera* meaning black. Long black tapering roots with top leaves distinguishable from those of salsify by their thinness. Its other name, equally apt, is 'viper's grass'. The flesh is reputedly tender and full of juice even when left in the ground for two years. Like salsify, it could be boiled, or its leaves eaten as salad.

At the base of the left-hand vegetable plot a row of Jerusalem artichokes had been marked flanking the pathway which divided it from the north wall border. This was a mixture of restoration and preservation. The artichokes already grew amongst the nettles, thrusting up tall every year, perennial successors of forgotten fathers. Other tall vegetables did have to be planted, including globe artichokes and asparagus, but they too could flank the sides of the two plots.

Mundane but useful parsnips, potatoes, onions, beans and peas were to run in descending order in rows of two or more down the right-hand plot. Towards the end of the plot the list became mildly more interesting by the addition of two rows of the celery-tasting root celeriac. This was included because it would also store and so could be used in the kitchen for seven or eight months of the year. If celeriac was interesting, then cardoons were positively riveting.

Cardoons? Apart from being prime candidates for articles on forgotten vegetables, what were they? In the old manuals they looked like sticks of celery. It was vaguely alarming to read that one fairly hefty woodcut illustration was an infinitesimal one-fifteenth of the real-life size of the vegetable. Cardoon stems could apparently reach a height of six-and-a-half feet (2 metres). They were also blessed with very large, feather-shaped grey-green leaves tipped with finely pointed yellow or brown spikes over half an inch (1 cm) long. Whatever could these dinosaurs have been used for?

Left: Salsify
Right: Celeriac
Far right: Cardoons

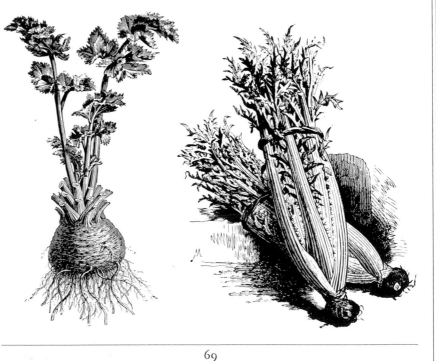

Harry knew. The giant stems were cut into small pieces and submerged into soups and stews. Harry had particular reason to recall cardoons. The vegetable had been grown in the kitchen garden of Stansted Park where he had started work as an improver journeyman when he was seventeen. When he became a head gardener, Harry remembered the cardoons at Stansted and decided to grow some at Chilton. It was only a small patch but the giants did so well that Harry entered them in the Royal Horticultural Society's show in London. He picked the patch over to select the best and was pleased when the entry caused quite a stir, no one had exhibited cardoons for years.

The garden at Chilton had always had a reputation for showing produce and, when Harry was taken on as head gardener, he was encouraged to keep this up but was warned 'what you show you will grow'. The morning after the London show, Harry received a visit at the garden from his employer asking to see the cardoon crop. Harry counted his lucky stars he still had enough left to constitute 'a crop'.

The last thing that still remained to be planned was the contents of the glasshouses. It was not a long job. It was obvious that even if the old water-heating boiler and four-inch-pipe (10-cm) system had been repairable, we could never afford to heat the houses as they had once been. One of the smaller houses had a central partition with a doorway leading from one side to the other. One half of this house would be ideal for cucumbers, the other half for melons. Tomatoes grown in another house would have to rely on natural warmth as the year progressed. The central 'show' house with steps up to its double door would also have to rely on the warmth of late spring and summer. In this natural warmth, we hoped sufficient flowers and plants would grow to grace the old iron-legged staging and perhaps reflect in the red-tiled floor a hint of the splendours the house had once held.

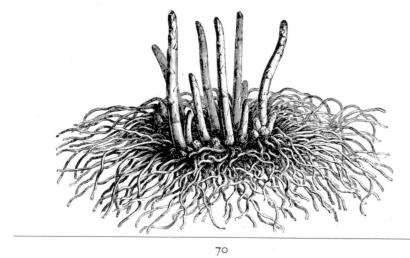

Left: Asparagus crown

CHAPTER SEVEN

•

Seeds lost and found – Controversy over confusion and unscrupulousness –
Potato blight or the Great Murrain.

W HERE was the wonderful Ringleader pea which could be brought to bear in May? Where the long, green-podded Prizetaker, or Lord Raglan, the finest wrinkled blue? Where the wonderful Ne Plus Ultra, the tall late marrow pea which helped bid goodbye to previous round-seeded peas as hard as buckshot? Where indeed were their sixty-seven companion varieties listed in Suttons' catalogue for 1866, or the astonishing a hundred and more varieties described in Mme Vilmorin-Andrieux's *The Vegetable Garden*: Dwarf, Longpodded, Giant, Prussian and Imperial? All had vanished from today's catalogues.

A circular letter to every known seed specialist in the country asking for their catalogue brought this depressing news. Catalogues received varied from those offering a mere ten pea varieties to larger firms managing a more heartening twenty-two. It was the same story for practically every category of vegetable. The enormous nineteenth-century diversity had become refined and narrowed to a few modern pedigree kinds.

As the intention was to plant up Chilton with old varieties it meant painstakingly cross-checking every modern seed catalogue against nineteenth-century lists to see if any of the old ones were still being sold. Of the peas, Gradus was still going strong and coming up for its centenary – having been certified by the Royal Horticultural Society in July 1887. Thomas Laxton was hard on its heels at eighty-eight years old. A few more, such as Alderman and Little Marvel, scraped in by virtue of having been introduced at the tail end of the Victorian period. In the columns of beans, the only runner bean which had stayed the course was Painted Lady, introduced in 1855. In Victorian catalogues this was also known as York and Lancaster Runner, because of its highly ornamental red and white blossoms.

Two decidedly venerable broad bean varieties appeared in every modern catalogue. Green Windsor, which came into being in 1831, and Aquadulce, which arrived from the Continent in the 1850s. Bunyard's Exhibition, although forty years younger than Aquadulce, seemed not to have lasted so well, appearing in only a few catalogues. The dwarf French bean Canadian Wonder prompted a question mark. Some sources stated it was introduced in 1873, but the Royal Horticultural Society records showed it had not been certified until 1903.

There was no doubt about some existing onion varieties. A fair number were definite centenarians. The Silver Skinned, White Spanish, White Lisbon, Paris Silver Skin, James' Long Keeping, Tree and Welsh onion are all pre-Victorian. Also still available, but not quite so venerable, were three introduced in the last years of the nineteenth century – the Bedfordshire Champion, the Oakey and Ailsa Craig. The latter is credited with causing a revolution in onion size. A grower in 1896 exhibited twelve specimens weighing thirty-seven and a half pounds (17 kilograms) – an enormous weight compared with early nineteenth-century onions. Amongst those which did not survive until today was an interesting brownish onion called Deptford, and the large, strong, fearsomely-named Blood-red, famous for its diuretic powers.

Of the brassicas, not one Victorian variety of Brussels sprout remained. It was a pity that we would not be able to see the old type at Chilton. Shirley Hibberd's 1881 description of them as 'tall military gentry with large buttons' made them seem particularly fetching. Of nineteenth-century broccoli, cauliflower-type varieties, Adam's Early White, Purple Cape, Late Queen and Leamington still remained, as did white and purple sprouting varieties.

Half a dozen or so old kinds of cabbage ranging from Winnigstadt, introduced in the 1860s, to Christmas Drumhead, in 1893, were still being sold. However, of the swollen thick-veined *Couve Tronchuda* (or Portugal cabbage), there was not a trace in any commercial seed catalogue we received. *Couve Tronchuda* had apparently tasted like a cross between cauliflower and seakale and had the wonderful virtue of not smelling cabbagy when cooked. We almost gave up hope of getting this paragon of a cabbage but Harry got in touch with a special 'contact' who sent him a small amount of seed. The old Early London, Snowball and Walcheren cauliflowers still existed but was today's Autumn Giant the same as Giant Autumn introduced by Mr Veitch in 1881? Of the fifteen varieties of borecole, as kale was then sometimes called, being offered in the 1866 catalogue, only three had survived – Green Curled, Cottager's and Ragged Jack. However, we later discovered that we had just missed Ragged Jack. The last commercial seed merchant to sell it had had his crop fail the year before.

Of the root vegetables, carrots had survived well. The Long Red Surrey and Early Horn date back as far as the 1830s, with French Forcing Horn and Nantes a legacy from the nineteenth-century growers. There was still, too, a good handful of Victorian radish varieties, although one, Wood's Early Frame, appeared in only one new seed catalogue. A slight confusion arose over parsnips. Our 1866 catalogue listed the still available Hollow Crown and the Student as separate varieties, but twenty years later Vilmorin-Andrieux's *The Vegetable Garden* had given the Student as just another name for Hollow Crown.

Feeling confused over variety names gave a certain historic authenticity to our seed ordering. It was apparently a state of mind fairly familiar to our ancestors when tackling the job. To go back to the pea, take for instance the confusing case of the Emerald Gem. In 1872 the Royal Horticultural Society asked Suttons whether their Suttons No. 1 Green and Suttons First of All were the same variety of pea as Suttons Emerald Gem. Suttons confirmed this was so and explained the reason for the thrice-named pea. They had submitted the pea as a novelty for trial to the Royal Horticultural Society at Chiswick under the provisional name No. 1 Green, however, on sending some more samples of the pea to the Royal Horticultural Society's gardens at Kensington, they called it Suttons First of All. Subsequently they discovered that they had a pea variety which cropped just as early, so decided a more fitting name would be Emerald Gem! Reverberations of the Emerald Gem confusion spilled into August of the following year. Mr Joseph Burgess of Knutsford wrote to the *Journal of Horticulture* to say that he thought its sending out was untradesmanlike. He had admired and approved of the variety for the last forty years knowing it under the name Rendall's Superb!

The famous horticultural journalist of the time, William Robinson, berated seed merchants for causing confusion by naming every good vegetable after themselves. He said they secured pure, well-selected stock of an old, good kind and rechristened it with their name followed by Champion or Favourite.

Muddying the waters of the nomenclature of vegetables by confusion was one thing. However, downright deception on the part of seed merchants was another. In the *Cottage Gardener* of 1852 there was reference to the *Gardener's Journal* accusing seed merchants of mixing dead seeds with live ones. The *Cottage Gardener* thought it unfair of the *Journal* to accuse the whole profession, advising their readers merely to

Above: Long carrot
Above left: White Spanish onion
Left: James's Long Keeping onion

avoid cheap seeds and deal only with respectable firms. Yet by 1866 things had evidently taken a turn for the worse. The Royal Horticultural Society published a report from the findings of a committee set up to enquire into the adulteration of seeds.

The report had been called for because of the unsatisfactory state of the seed trade and the bad quality of much of the seed being sold to the public. Complaints had been made that purchasers of seed frequently received neither the kind nor quality they had paid for and had no remedy against this except a chancy and expensive lawsuit.

Harry in his office checking the first batches of seed to arrive

The committee confirmed that dealers kept seed too long and sold it after it had lost its vitality; that they added bad seed to good and mixed old with new; also that they manipulated and doctored bad seed to make it look good by dyeing, sulphur-smoking or oil-dressing it. One informant told the committee about a firm whose principal business was destroying the vitality of cheap seeds to mix with sound seeds of greater value. The committee members purchased various packets of seed anonymously from eighteen seed dealers in London. From each dealer they bought one packet each of the five commonest vegetables: cauliflower, broccoli, carrots and white and yellow turnips. In each packet were one hundred seeds. The committee planted each of the eighteen packets, variety by variety, and recorded in the case of each dealer how many seeds had come up.

Of the cauliflower seeds the highest germination was eighty-six for one packet, the other packets followed in descending order with the lowest down to only twenty-four. For broccoli the highest was eighty-six and the lowest thirty-five. Carrots were marginally better, with the highest packet producing ninety-eight plants and the lowest fifty-seven. Results for white turnip were also reasonable but for yellow turnip the success rate plummeted from ninety-five down to twenty-eight.

The report concluded that the government should attempt to protect 'the very large numbers of ignorant and uneducated people who have to purchase seeds', pointing out that in Prussia government experts were appointed to test the quality of seed.

In the light of all this it might well have been advisable for gardeners to save and collect seed from their own crops. Many did, storing them in canvas bags or in brown paper made from old ships' ropes which smelt repellent enough to keep insects at bay. Doing this could, however, lead back to the nomenclature muddle. Without the aid of botanical science, seeds from parent plants, stored and then resown, frequently illustrated the fact of nature that anything propagated by seed changes its characteristics every generation. For example, a man with five children will pass on different characteristics to each child.

Even a man with twenty or a hundred children will not pass on *exactly* the same genes to any two of his children – a different mixture is scooped out of the father's gene reservoir each time. By the next generation, it's all different again. In the same way, vegetable seed sown from the previous year's crop came up slightly differently. The difference was compounded by pests, weather and disease, all playing a part in altering the plant's appearance. It is hardly surprising that some old varieties might still keep their original name with some gardeners but with others be known by entirely new names.

Another reason for the proliferation of vegetable names was that some varieties suited the soil in some areas of the country, while elsewhere a different variety was to be preferred. This was due to nature's own process of selection. Being grown in the same place year after year, the variety had adapted to the soil or climatic conditions and produced a good crop. Naturally, gardeners and growers concentrated on sowing these particular varieties and they became known by the name of the area. For example, Altrincham carrots, Norfolk turnips, Bedford Brussels sprouts and Yorkshire Hero peas.

So much for the reasons for the seemingly wide range of Victorian vegetable varieties but what had brought about the comparable paucity of vegetables on offer in our new seed catalogues? One of the reasons was no doubt the modern need to produce a vegetable as a commercial commodity, of a uniform size so that it could be harvested mechanically, and suitable for freezing. The extinct type of Brussels sprout developed unevenly, starting at the bottom first. This would not be acceptable to a twentieth-century commercial grower who needs the whole of his crop ready at the same time for ease of harvesting and in order to meet contracts. Experiments were made to try to achieve what growers wanted. Scientists took the old variable characteristics and narrowed them down, figuratively pouring them all through a narrow funnel, leaving only the characteristics which would ensure uniformity.

This was the beginning of D.U.C. – Distinct, Uniform and Constant – which is what every new variety today has to be and a far cry from its Victorian ancestor which is politely known as 'variable'. D.U.C. is a form of consumer protection test which tries to ensure that your seeds will crop on time, have the colour and size that you expect, and that a packet of the same variety sown in another year will be identical.

When Britain joined the Common Market in 1973 it was a requirement that all vegetable varieties should be D.U.C., and a National List was made of vegetables which met the required standard. This list was also seen as a means of avoiding the massive legacy of confusing synonyms and of helping the seed trade rationalise by not having to carry so many different varieties. If a vegetable is not on the National List it is illegal to sell it.

To many people the going to the wall (and not the garden one) of many of the old interesting varieties in sacrifice to commercial economy, is deplored as a sad loss of variety and flavour in life. The Ministry of Agriculture does point out, however, that if someone is prepared to carry out all the required tests on an old variety and to maintain it so that it keeps true, it can be added to the National List. Apparently not many do this, although there are a few people prepared to go to great lengths to keep the old varieties alive. Hence the appearance of 'Vegetable Sanctuaries', in which old varieties are grown and from which seeds are issued to interested gardeners looking for something more than D.U.C.

In a bed of thoroughbred modern vegetables all crop together, on time and when expected, but that does have one drawback – with their narrow base of characteristics, what kills one can kill them all. On the other hand, although cold and disease might have affected a Victorian crop, it was made up of such diverse individuals that some would almost certainly have struggled through. Ironically, this valuable richness of characteristics which contributed to their variability and downfall is the reason for the survival of many Victorian varieties today. At what is probably their last bastion, the National Vegetable Research Station near Stratford-on-Avon, seeds from the old vegetables are kept in a seed bank. Here, if needs be, their characteristics can be dipped into to help breed better new varieties, or to help out when today's vegetables run into problems with disease or pests and need reinforcing.

A visit to the seed bank revealed the elusive old Ragged Jack kale growing in a small but healthy quantity in a corner of one of the glasshouses. Not far away was a crop of lettuce which had red blotches over its leaves. The lettuce, obviously not for the squeamish, was called Bloody Warrior, the red blotches supposedly being the blood spots from fallen heroic warriors. It had been donated by the last man left growing it.

The seed bank receives many donations – from airmail letters containing foreign seed to single faded packets found at the backs of drawers by people clearing out houses. Even if only one or two seeds germinate from the old packets, the Research Station can cosset these to grow and reproduce more.

The process of obtaining more seed is something of a surprise to the unbotanically minded. Glasshouses and polythene tunnels, usually associated with forming cover over neat, immaculately-cultivated plants, house instead a variety of strange triffid-like vegetables which

Title page and cover from an early Sutton's seed catalogue

have been encouraged to 'bolt' skywards and break into flower. Once in flower, a large bowl of embryo blowflies is placed in amongst them and the area sealed up. The blowflies hatch and fly on to the flowers. They crawl over them, going from plant to plant, pollinating the vegetables as they go. The flies then die, having had a short but ecstatic life. The ecstasy is multiplied for those epicurean flies lucky enough to have pollinated onion flowers – a particular delicacy.

After the seeds have ripened comes drying, then the flower heads are 'threshed' to remove the seed. Painstaking care is taken to obtain as wide a selection of seed from each plant as possible. A commercial producer might disregard all the small seeds and keep only the large ones but here the idea is to be able to have as many permutations of the plant make-up as possible. There may well be some characteristic in the small seed which isn't present in the large, and vice versa.

From a drying room, the seeds are put into metal foil packets and placed alongside hundreds of other packets in a walk-in cold store. The temperature inside the cold store is minus 4 degrees Fahrenheit ($-20°$C). Every so often, samples of seed are removed from the store and sown to check that there has been no deterioration. The seeds should last in the cold store for fifty years, but as the genebank is only six years old the theory has yet to be proved.

It would have been splendid to have had some seed from the old Victorian varieties in the genebank but the bank is an international reservoir funded by OXFAM. These old varieties will remain suspended into the next century as an insurance policy against climatic disaster and disease.

The British Queen was diseased. She was suffering from a last-century legacy of climatic disaster and disease which even the genebank could not have helped – that unconquered murrain, the blight.

The British Queen is one of 350 potato varieties grown by Donald Maclean at his farm in Perthshire. Mr Maclean believes it to be the largest private collection of potatoes in the world. He promotes and tries to keep alive old varieties which have fallen by the wayside, despite their good flavours, because their knobbly shape, yield and sometimes even colour, which could be an interesting purple or blue, does not suit today's commercial world.

For the early crop potatoes to be brought on under coldframes in the walled garden, we had ordered Epicure, Duke of York, Ninetyfold and Eclipse from Donald Maclean. These antiquarians were thriving and available, as were maincrop varieties, Magnum Bonum and Fortyfold, which were destined for the central vegetable plot. However, of the 'second earlies', ordered for the warm south border and planned to fill the gap between early and maincrop, only Edzell Blue was available. British Queen would have to be substituted by International Kidney.

Being told that British Queen had blight was rather like seeing a ripple hitting the sides of a pond today – the turbulent epicentre of that ripple stretching back to 1845.

In that year, on 16 August, a Doctor Salter wrote in the *Gardeners' Chronicle* of a disease which had been affecting potatoes in the south of England since July. So rapid and devastating was the progress of the disease through the country that a fortnight after its first recorded appearance, few sound potatoes could be found at Covent Garden Market. At the beginning of September the disease was recorded as having appeared in Scotland and Ireland, where it went on to have such devastating results.

The disease had been prevalent in the United States in 1844, and was described as taking the following form. The potato plants would look in the peak of health with their leaves particularly lush and green but, within a few days, black spots would appear on the leaves. The leaves would then wither, blacken and putrefy, falling on to the earth in an offensive mess. The rot then spread to the potato tubers and the entire plant would give off a disgusting odour. So rapid and fatal was the disease that in a few days it would spread from plant to plant over a large tract and, in less than a week, turn every stem and leaf in the field to one rotten mass. The seriousness of the situation prompted the governments of Europe to issue commissions to examine the disease and try to find a remedy.

It became increasingly difficult to obtain sound seed potatoes. Every newspaper in the country carried stories of the disease. People wrote in to say it was like an epidemic resembling cholera, particularly the smell. Others variously attributed its cause to microscopic insects, to railways, to electrical influences, to the animal manure used in planting and to the breakdown of the potato plant through over-cultivation. Being the age of charades and pantomimes, the potato quickly appeared on stage. A giant tuber was carried surmounted by a giant aphis. This was referred to as the 'Aphis Vast-tater'. The Aphis vastator was, according to Mr Alfred Smee, Surgeon to the Bank of England, the reason for the potato disease. He held the view that an aphid settled on the leaves of the potato, puncturing them and making them susceptible to an attack of the disease.

The correct diagnosis was finally made following the studies of the Reverend M. J. Berkeley and his colleagues. They attributed the lush-ness of the potato foliage prior to the onset of the disease becoming apparent, to the mycelium of a fungus which provoked the green colouring matter in the leaves. The mycelium then threaded its way destructively through the tissues of the leaves and down the stem to the tubers in the ground. The fungus was known as *Peronospora infestans*. It was seen as being analogous to a bad attack of croup in humans as it caused the leaves' breathing pores to become completely choked up.

Although the fungus had been identified, no cure could be found. Dull, close and foggy weather was feared, as it seemed to favour the disease. Each year, regular geographical reports appeared on the murrain. In early August 1871, the weather in the Midland districts was reported as being warm and unsettled. The potato disease appeared amongst the second earlies and everything indicated it would develop its full virulence amongst the late crops, should August turn out wet and warm. At the same time in the Vale of Gloucester, things were worse – the smell of the potatoes showed that the fungus was spreading very fast and many people were already complaining of dry, diseased plants.

It was believed that too rich a soil produced potato foliage gorged with crude sap. The sap required hot and dry weather in order that the plant could digest it properly. In dull, close weather, the necessary digestion could not take place and the sap went unprocessed directly down to the tubers and formed a fitting medium for the spores of the fungus. Whatever the cause, no remedy could be found. Two potato varieties, Sutton's Red-skin Flourball and Skerry Blue, proved to have the most resistance to blight, but the Flourball did not have a good flavour. There was not one variety which proved to be completely immune. It was this fact which probably started an interest in breeding to improve the 'noble tuber'.

William Paterson, a potato breeder from Dundee, sent orders to America and Australia in an effort to find fresh disease-free stock. In 1863 John Nicoll bred a variety called Champion. It appeared to have a certain amount of resistance to blight, probably because of its late maturity. The seed merchants Carters sent £10,000 worth of Champion to the stricken Irish potato growers.

James Clarke, a gardener from Hampshire, bred three of the potatoes we had ordered from Donald Maclean – Magnum Bonum, which was also at first not so susceptible to blight because of its late maturity, Epicure and Ninetyfold.

In the 1870s it was said to be a disgrace to science and to scientific men that no perfect remedy had been found for the potato disease. Almost 120 years later there is still no perfect remedy but that is not for the want of trying. The fight has been a chequered one. At first a copper sulphate-based concoction known as Bordeaux Mixture was used. It was the same spray used for treating mildew on vines. Then, at the beginning of this century, a major advance was made when a wild potato called *Solanum dermissum* was found in Mexico and proved to be blight-resistant. Experiments started to hybridise this wild variety with domestic stock. At first it seemed as though the resultant seedlings were also blight-resistant but it proved to be only a temporary lull in the cold war between man and the blight. By the 1930s the disease was attacking the previously resistant stock. Scientists found that the fungus was always one jump ahead, and by the 1940s realised their work was getting them nowhere. They changed tactics and began to work on 'field resistance', concentrating on slowing down the growth of blight rather than on producing a potato which was completely immune. They could do this because the new breeds had a great many more genes giving greater resistance and acting as a buffer against the disease. Most potatoes bred today are field resistant but it is still essential, particularly during wet summers, to combine the fight against blight with sprays. Today a tin-based spray has replaced the old copper sulphate one.

Blight-banished nineteenth-century potatoes may be making a come-back – or at least relevant parts of them. The Plant Breeding Institute at Cambridge has a dozen or so old potato varieties at which they are looking. They believe that the old varieties may be able to help on three scores. One is to help meet the demands of supermarket and other commercial entrepreneurs who say that today's customers are looking for more and different flavour in potatoes. The Friends of the Earth and anyone concerned about chemical pollution might be pleased to know the second reason for the old varieties' resurrection. When they were originally grown, low levels of fertilisers were used and the potatoes seemed to grow well enough. Today, new varieties have been selected to respond to more and more chemicals. Could it be that with the help of the old potatoes new varieties could be bred which would grow at lower levels of chemical input?

The third reason for renewed interest is that when Victorian potato varieties were being grown, many of today's viruses were unknown. Perhaps the old varieties have a resistance to twentieth-century viruses which scientists have missed?

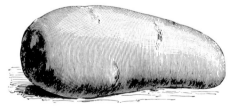

CHAPTER EIGHT

•

Icehouses and hotbeds – Putting fruit trees 'Early to bed, early to rise' –
The complexities of pruning –How a Morello cherry became
a life benefit.

DESPITE searches, old estate plans showing the grounds around our restored walled garden never revealed the whereabouts of an ice-house. It is certainly likely there had been one once, for ice-houses were seen as necessities, particularly in the affluent nineteenth century. They acted as larders for fish, game, poultry and butter and throughout the summer months supplied ice for cooling drinks and for exotic desserts.

Filling the ice-house one day in winter was the responsibility of the head gardener. From contemporary accounts the day the ice-house was filled must have been as traditional and exciting as the day the first cut of corn was made in summer. Head gardeners could, befitting their status, call up a substantial work-force for the job. Some men were required to wield barbed hooks on the end of poles, others supplied with stout clubs to smash the ice into pieces and still others stood by with hayforks waiting to load the ice into a cart.

Ice for the ice-house had to be at least two inches (5 cm) thick and as clear as crystal. If it had leaves or broken twigs in it it would not 'keep'. To retrieve ice from the middle of a pond, a clubman and a hooker were rowed out, the clubman to hit off a chunk of ice and the hooker to harpoon it and drag it back behind the boat. As it is fairly certain that thermal gloves would not have been much in evidence on the day, it is heartening to know that some establishments provided the men with a large can of home-brew straight from a fire and with ginger grated into it.

A horse-drawn cart carried the ice from the pond to the ice-house. In some cases, ice-houses were built close enough to the pond for ice to be transferred by hand. The remains of the two ice-houses in the grounds of Chatsworth House are only a stone's throw from their respective ponds.

The design for ice-houses and other structures to preserve ice varied over the years. Plans for ice-houses were recorded as early as the 1660s. By the nineteenth century a 'successful' ice-house was being described as twenty feet deep from the crown of its dome to the bottom, eleven feet wide near the top and five feet near the base (6 × 3·3 × 1·5 metres).

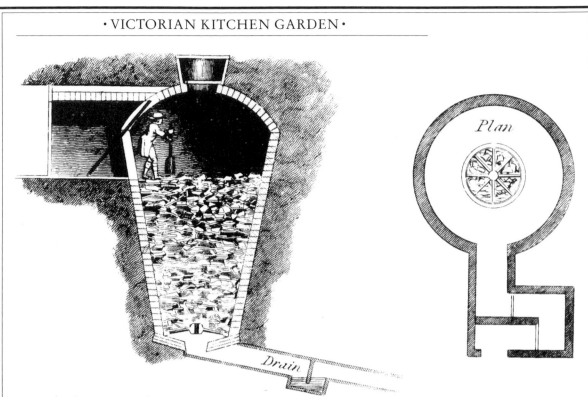

Plan

Drain

It was built into the side of a hill. This design was credited with keeping ice up to a thickness of ten feet (3 metres) as late as September.

Ice from the pond was pounded and tipped through a hole at the top of the house. When sufficient was stored, a wooden lid was put over the hole and the lid covered in coal ashes to throw off rain and snow water. A drain in the base of the house kept the structure from flooding, which was essential to preserve the ice. Excluding air was also thought very necessary. The side passageway and door providing access to the stored ice were blocked off with straw. Such was the preoccupation with keeping out air, that some ice-house owners even went to the lengths of having a series of long passages built with intermediate doors and plastered the chinks of the doors with mortar.

At one time salt was added to the ice with the thought that, like salted beef, it would keep longer. This proved unsuccessful. There was a continual controversy over whether or not ice-houses benefited by having shady trees planted over them, or indeed whether they needed to be underground at all. Robert Fortune, the plant collector, returned from China and reported that in that warm country ice was kept stacked above ground and covered with a thick coat of thatch. This prompted the ice-stack or 'iceberg' to become common from the mid-1840s but a large number of stack failures caused people to go back to the original pit designs.

Above: Diagrams showing passages leading to an ice-house and how the ice was stored
Right: Illustrations from a handbook for builders published in 1874. The removal of the glass tax in 1845 brought glasshouses and the luxury of forced produce to many gardens

It was known that 'chemical science' could manufacture ice. However, the expense involved in providing sufficient ice in this way to meet the demands of a society used to and demanding large amounts of this particular luxury was too prohibitive for many households. The responsibility remained with the head gardener to choose an appropriate day and fill the ice-house.

He had also in winter months to put his mind to providing other luxuries, mostly from the kitchen garden. This *was* something we could try to tackle.

John Ruskin, who believed that every climate gave its vegetable food to its living creatures at the right time, called 'forcing' a vile and gluttonous modern habit. Mistress Margaret Dods, in her *Cook and Housewife's Manual* of 1826, referred to it as a vanity which spurred people on to load their tables with flavourless, colourless, immature vegetables. She did concede that whereas in years gone by a turnip, a cabbage or a leek was the only vegetable luxury found on a country gentleman's table, there was beginning a regular succession not merely of broccoli, cauliflower and peas, but of the more recondite asparagus, seakale, endive and artichoke, with an abundance of small salading.

As the musty account book in Harry's garden office had shown, during the winter months at the turn of the century the custom of forcing vegetables had still been flourishing at Chilton. Harry himself remembered sowing carrots on 19 January which would be ready for the dining-room in April.

There was a variety of methods for forcing: on hotbeds of fermenting manure and leaves; in dark forcing sheds; under frames, handlights and terracotta pots; and inside warm glasshouses and pits.

Harry planned to make a row of hotbeds below the patch of Prince Albert rhubarb. It would mean obtaining a considerable amount of horse-dung. This at first posed a problem. The stable block built next to the walled garden had not seen a horse for over half a century. The problem was resolved when it was found that Wally, the builder who had repaired the coldframes, had a daughter who kept ponies. It also meant knocking up some boards to support the lights needed to cover each bed.

Making a hotbed required preparation. Once a sufficiently large heap of stable dung was obtained it had to be wetted, if it was dry, and turned over four or five times for at least a fortnight. This 'working well' stopped the manure becoming too hot and jeopardising the operation from the start by burning the roots of any plant placed in it.

Above: Coldframes
Below: Hotbeds are given a prominent position in this engraving of useful garden devices

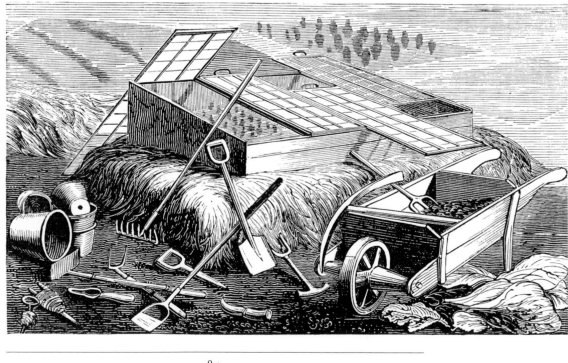

Mixing leaves with the manure helped to moderate the heat. The next job was measuring the frame and marking out corresponding measurements for the bed, allowing an extra sixteen inches (40 cm) more each way. The easiest way to do this was to drive four stakes into the ground to serve as a guide. The dung was then shaken up, placed between the stakes and beaten down with a fork. Beating down was important, it compacted the manure and ensured a controlled slow release of heat.

When the manure was built up to three feet (1 metre), the frame and lights went on top. Five days had then to go by to allow rank steam to escape from the bed. On day six, a layer of good loamy soil was put under each light. Following a Victorian recipe for sweetening the soil, Harry added some powdered chalk to the bed destined to provide Early Horn carrots, a short-rooted variety developed especially to grow in the shallow soil of hotbeds. By next day the manure beneath had

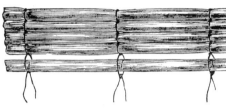

warmed the soil sufficiently for planting. Provided that they were kept at 70 degrees Fahrenheit (21·C) by lining with fresh dung and by making sure they were covered over in cold weather, hotbeds could be kept in production for a considerable time.

Although we were making our hotbeds in January, some gardeners who wanted, say, cucumbers at Christmas, would have started their plants on a hotbed in early October. Salading, cabbage and potatoes could all be raised on hotbeds. When potatoes were planted, radish seed could also be scattered on to the same hotbed. If this was in January, the radishes would be ready for pulling in March and the potatoes for digging in May. In the nineteenth century the blight made potatoes scarce and often, when their price rose above that of bread, unobtainable to the poor, so early potatoes were a particular delicacy. As well as being raised on hotbeds, they were forced in frames heated by flues and covered with bleached calico painted with a mixture of boiled oil and sugar of lead.

Above: Straw mat used to protect frames from frost Below: Radish

Peas, deemed the 'Prince' of Victorian vegetables, were worth the effort of forcing for out-of-season appearance on the dining-table. The best way was by coddling them in the borders of a peach house or growing single plants in pots, transferring the pots in succession to warm houses. Onions sown in boxes and put into vineries could be pulled throughout the winter if sowings were made every fortnight.

Dwarf kidney beans did well in pineapple houses. They were robust enough to withstand the 80 degrees Fahrenheit (27°C) given to the pines during the winter months. Kidney beans were the only additional plants advised for pineapple houses and even they had to be grown in the house from seed. This was a sensible precaution when you consider that mealy bug and scale were so feared that gardeners examined pineapple leaves with magnifying glasses in order to stop the pests in time.

Owing to the defunct heating system at the garden we could no longer rely on putting pots of vegetables into the glasshouses for forcing, but we could try the other methods.

Forcing seakale under terracotta pots was viewed in 1857 as effective but costly. This was because pots cost from 2s 6d to 3s 6d (12p to 17p) and could be easily broken with a fork. The seakale pot we bought from a pottery, quite a rarity as not many are now made, cost £18. In addition to this we bought one from an antique shop which required sticking together, had one donated by a head gardener friend of Harry's and one Harry had had tucked away for some years. There was also another which had languished for a considerable time in the north border but when it was turned over it was found to have only one side.

The price of our one rhubarb pot, albeit an interesting and, we were told, particularly old funnel-shape, had also escalated (if it was 3s 6d when new) by an awesome 6000 per cent. 'Gardenalia' was, it seemed, taking profitable roots in the same commercial bosoms that had furthered pine tables and 'kitchenalia'.

Going back to seakale, Harry proposed forcing it in traditional but different ways. One method was to wait until the frosts on the east-facing border made the curly silver leaves wither. When this happened, one pot could cover three plants. Once in place, the pots themselves would have to have a good fifteen inches (38 cm) of manure heaped round each one to provide the necessary warmth and protection needed to encourage the dormant crowns inside to shoot. We intended to ignore certain garden writers of the past who considered this manure covering 'offensive to delicate olfactory nerves', and recommended the operation taking place behind the garden in an out-of-the-way place. Forced in this way, seakale could be ready for cutting a month to five weeks after the pot had been put on.

Forced seakale

The usefulness of seakale was especially appreciated when severe weather destroyed broccoli and other greens, or made them so scarce that they could not be sent to the house every day. Forced seakale could supply the family from the end of December to the end of May. As a belt-and-braces insurance for a continued supply, the other method Harry intended to follow was to take up several crowns, remove the 'thongs' from them to heel in for rooting for further crops, and then to put the crowns themselves into the north border. When they were well chilled, he proposed to take up the crowns, put them in boxes of loam and place the boxes into a warm, dark place. This would encourage the white shoots. The same method could be used for Witloof chicory, which would be planted in succession from October to February, and also for asparagus. Asparagus could, however, have its own forcing beds. The ones at the Royal Gardens at Frogmore were particularly grand. They were seventy-five feet long and seven feet wide (23 × 2 metres). The lower half of the beds were filled with rich soil and the upper half had a flow and return pipe of hot water connected to a boiler. Forcing started in December and the asparagus was ready for cutting by the end of the same month.

In addition to being forced outside under manure-covered pots, rhubarb could also be forced in mushroom houses. The insulated mushroom house at Chilton had decayed too far to be resurrected but mushrooms would, it seemed, flourish in a variety of places. According to the old manuals they could be put into the beds recently vacated by melons, the spawn having been inserted while the melons were still growing; on to shelves at the back of forcing houses and sometimes into open borders, although the time of eventual appearance in the border could be an uncertain matter. Mushroom beds could remain productive for a month to six weeks. With sufficient room, other beds could be started to follow on in succession. By this method an almost constant supply could be kept up. Harry plumped for spawning a hotbed in a mat-darkened frame to see if he could raise an early crop.

Above: Mushrooms
Below: Three-quarter span vinery

If the methods of keeping parsley, lettuce and endive come under 'forcing', then they should be mentioned here. Parsley for garnishing and lettuce, particularly the Bath Brown Cos for salad, we intended to keep protected during winter by lantern handlights. There would be other lettuce too, including Lamb's lettuce under coldframes. Also under coldframes, protected by mats, would be endive, which when tied up with bast would lose its bitterness and blanch to a bright delicate yellow.

In the days when the upright tubular boiler had turned the massive iron piping around each glasshouse into warm arteries, winter forcing would not have been confined to vegetables. The peach, apricot and fig houses, the early vinery and cherry and plum houses, would each play their part in the skilful and exacting business of coaxing fruit buds from trees which, left to their own devices, would have remained dormant until the following spring.

On Christmas Eve at Chilton the peach house had always been 'started' with an eye to getting peaches ready for picking by mid-May. On the same day the early vine house was closed up in the hope that there would be grapes ripe in the first ten days of June. The second peach house was 'started' a month later but instead of a month's gap between the first and second house fruiting, as the spring advanced the second house caught up sufficiently to be ready to take over as soon as the first house finished.

It was all part of a carefully-managed cycle. To be able to provide fruit two months or more earlier than its normal season, the head gardener had to think ahead and adhere to the old maxim 'Early to bed, early to rise...' If, as in some gardens, fruit forcing started early in autumn, then the trees needed to have rested in the summer. After fruit had been gathered in May or June, the lights on the fruit houses were removed and the trees aired. In August or September they were pruned and their branches scrubbed with a brush and water and 'done over' with a mixture of sulphur, soft soap and tobacco liquid or a similar composition of sulphur, clay, cow-dung and soot. Borders were forked up and six inches (15 cm) of old soil replaced by turfy maiden loam. All the trellis and woodwork in the houses had to be washed with soap and water, every wall whitewashed and the hot-water pipes painted with a mixture of equal parts lime and sulphur.

Aired, rested and lulled by the approach of autumn into dormancy, trees would have to be coaxed into activity. One way of doing this was to syringe them over twice a day with water heated to 50 degrees Fahrenheit (10°C). Once the sap began to rise, it had to be kept going. If the tree lapsed back into dormancy the chances were high that further attempts at forcing it would fail. Heat started off slowly, nothing over 45 degrees Fahrenheit (7°C) in the first month. The boiler was stoked up every evening, soon after sunset, with sufficient fuel to last through the night and renewed in the morning. If the management was good, blossom buds swelled and forcing would begin in earnest. As the *Book of Garden Management* of 1862 eloquently put it: 'From the time the bud bursts its horny sheath until the luscious fruit melts in your mouth, all work and no play – all growth and no check, must be the stern regimen of the successful cultivator.'

Fires continued until May, with care not to raise the temperature above 60 degrees Fahrenheit (16°C) in peach and cherry houses and above 70 degrees (21°C) in vine houses. Cherries could be ready for picking as early as April and grapes, plums, apricots and peaches in May and June.

The earliest fruit could be obtained from trees grown in pots which had received the additional benefit of being thrust into heated beds of bark or dung in the forcing houses. By having peach trees in pots and putting them into a heated vinery, a gardener could avoid the risk of harming his larger trees by too severe forcing. A Mr Hutchinson of Eatington Park in Warwickshire was recorded as having ripened peaches in pots as early as the first week in April.

Gooseberries, raspberries and currants could also be potted up and brought on in glasshouses. Raspberries could be ripe at the beginning of April. Figs under glass could also be brought to ripen in April and kept in production until November. The best way of being able to pick strawberries on Christmas Day was to follow the plan adopted by gardeners in Copenhagen. They sowed Alpine strawberry seeds in July and August, put any resultant strong plants in pots, then forced the plants slowly in pits with pitched roofs.

Our restored but heatless Victorian glasshouses could not aspire to strawberries on Christmas Day – although they had once, and not so very many years ago, been able to provide ripe strawberries in April. Harry recalled how in late autumn, potted strawberry 'runners' which had been left in a cool unused house during the summer to form firm-crowned young plants, were taken to the potting shed. The journeyman or apprentice scooped out an inch (2·5 cm) or more of soil from the top of each pot then knocked the plant completely out of the pot to make sure all the roots and drainage crocks in the base were clear. If they were, he put the plant back into the pot and refilled the sides and top with rich loam. The fresh loam had to be rammed down tightly. When he had finished, the foreman came along to carry out the traditional test. He picked up the strawberry plant by its leaves and vigorously swung it backwards and forwards. If the pot and the plant did not part company, he was satisfied that the loam had been packed in tightly enough. If the pot went flying off in the opposite direction and he was left holding up a bunch of quivering roots, things were not so bright for the apprentice.

The first batch of top-dressed strawberry pots was put into a warm peach or vine house before Christmas. The pots were placed on a shelf high up on the back wall near the glass roof. Further pots went into other peach houses and vineries as each house was 'started'. This kept up a constant supply to the dining-room from April until the first strawberries under cloches in the garden were ready. The strawberries under cloches were followed during summer by those in open beds. The open-bed strawberries were followed in the early autumn by the small Alpine strawberries and, for real one-upmanship, although Harry cannot remember it being done in his day, there was the Copenhagen method for strawberries at Christmas.

No longer able to rely on the peach houses and vineries for winter warmth, Harry decided to raise a few early strawberries on a hotbed. It was a method that had been employed a century ago and although he had never tried it, Harry was game to experiment.

In the meantime the old peach houses could not be forgotten. One of them still provided cool shelter to several peach and nectarine trees. The trees had been trained to 'fan' shapes, and January was the traditional time for winter pruning and tying-in. Translated, this meant to cut off the dead wood which had borne fruit last season and to tie-in young shoots formed last summer which would eventually bear fruit.

Harry's long experience had taught him that as every tree differed, the approach to pruning had to be equally varied. Textbooks, describing the process, were not a great deal of help. Mawe's *Everyman His Own Gardener* (our edition was printed in 1845) spent six pages on pruning; the instructions are painstaking, thorough and as clear as whitewashed glass. A novice confronted with a shoot-covered tree and the following advice could be forgiven for uncertainty. If there was not room to lay-in more than one of the, say, three shoots produced from the branches laid-in last winter, then he must:

Below: Pruning knife (left) and garden knife Right: Patent American tree pruner

Cut off the lower one quite close to the branch, and then that part of the branch which hath the upper shoot upon it must be pruned down to the middle one; so that there is only the middle shoot remaining, which terminates or makes the end of the branch; but, if it is thought most convenient to leave the uppermost of the three, the middle and lower to be cut away, or on the contrary, if the lower shoot only to be left, to cut off the branch with the middle and upper shoot, close to the lower one or if thought proper to leave two out of three shoots then the upper and lower, etc, etc. . .

Mawe might have turned out a few excellent pruners but it is hardly surprising that most garden apprentices learned by watching the foreman or head gardener. Let loose to prune and tie-in by themselves, they then had their work inspected and were often made to undo and painstakingly re-tie to the head gardener's satisfaction. It was all a question of balance and pride. A well-tied tree could be a thing of beauty to behold in a winter garden.

For tying-in the shoots, worn strips from common garden mats were recommended as these would break as the branch thickened and not cut into it. Harry had always used a hank of bast. He fixed it like a large yellow horse-tail on to the side of the fruit-house ladder. Unlike normal ladders, those in use in the fruit house had two protruding pieces tacked on to the upper end. These two stilts of wood effectively raised the rungs from the wall and prevented them from damaging the tree beneath.

Pruning and tying was, said Harry, a question of keeping an 'eye forward'. In other words you always had to look ahead to see where you were going. It was no use cutting out branches and then discovering that the tree's shape was out of balance because at one point, either to left or right, there were not enough young shoots to cover a gap.

Harry was against 'poaching' on a tree. This means to leave a great many fruit spurs on a tree in order to obtain a good show of peaches. He believed that this overburdened a tree. The other point about short-fruiting spurs was that they could only be left on once a tree had been balanced. If the tree was still young, it was better to concentrate on getting the longer branches to grow at the right angle.

To prune properly it was necessary to untie the tree from the wall wires. In order to achieve a good spread-out fan shape you had, when you tied the tree back to the wall, to pull the branches down and outwards, leaving a three- to five-inch (8- to 12-cm) gap between each branch or rib of the fan. This improved the shape of the fan and also prevented too much top growth by stopping the sap rushing straight up. It was the same principle used in vine houses where, after pruning, vine rods were tied down to check their growth.

'Tie a young piece of wood over an old piece but not vice versa' was the instruction to follow. In tying, neatness was paramount. Neat 'butterfly' bows were needed to secure the shoots to the wall wires and there was another trick which had been passed on down the years. If you wanted to support or straighten a long side branch by fastening it to a branch above or below it, you knotted a piece of bast over the branch then, before tying it to the other branch, you held the bast out and twisted it between finger and thumb, like hand-spinning. This simple method made the bast thinner and less visible. It also stopped it spreading out to an obtrusive untidy size, the width of a pruning-knife handle, when it became wet after the tree had been syringed.

There was also a row of fig trees to be pruned and tied-in in much the same way, but the fig shoots had to have looser ties as they were more vigorous. What none of the old books mentioned about pruning fig trees and what Harry had found out by experience over the years, was always to prune from the bottom up. This stopped sap falling on to hands and arms. At first the sap seemed harmless enough but when it dried it contracted on the skin and caused itching and burning.

The same pruning and tying-in would have to be done soon on the young fan-trained peach and nectarine trees on the south-facing wall of the garden and on the sweet cherries on the east-facing wall. There were also the two Morello cherries against the centre of the north-facing wall. Tying-in Morello cherry trees had a profound effect on one Victorian gardener. The tale is told by a Mr Ross of Surbiton in the *Journal of Horticulture* for November 1872:

The late Mr. Hector Rose was my last apprentice in Scotland. Soon after his settlement in Windsor he came to see me, for which I thanked him, expressing my gratification that in his rare success he did not forget me. 'Oh!' he replies, 'did you expect that I could forget you and the Morello Cherry tree that you made me unnail after I finished nailing it? You then said that if I could not train properly I must give up nailing altogether. Nor was this all; you used to tell visitors who admired it that it was trained by the youngest apprentice. Now sir, had you given me £100 that day I should have benefited comparatively little by it, but unnailing that tree was to me a life benefit. I made men unnail trees more than fifty times, hoping they also would find it good for them. I cannot express my gratitude to you for your pointedness on my first start in the world.'

CHAPTER NINE

•

*Grafting the 'Maltster' – Thomas Rivers, a nurseryman who
raised his own memorials.*

*Right: Scion
Below: Stock*

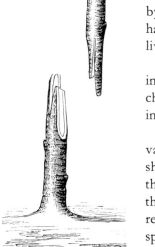

THE time had come to go back to the National Apple Collection at Brogdale in Kent and take a graft from the Victorian apple, the Maltster. This was the excellent culinary apple described by Hogg in his *Fruit Manual* so lovingly that it seemed a pity that it had become forgotten by the fruit world. It is now a museum specimen living at Brogdale as a curiosity, the last survivor of its race.

The Maltster's re-entry into the outside world, its first step being into our walled garden, had been planned the previous autumn. The chosen method of propagation, through grafting, had to be carried out in March or April when the sap was beginning to rise.

Gardeners who planned to graft to obtain more trees of a certain variety thought well ahead. Months prior to grafting, they cut the shoots, or scions, from the trees they wanted to propagate and laid them in the cool north border of the walled garden. If covered for two-thirds of their length with soil, the scions would remain healthy until ready for grafting on to a root-bearing trunk (or stock) the following spring.

A scion had been removed from the Maltster for us and kept at Brogdale as it seemed simplest to graft it there on to one of their root-stocks. Modern grafting involves joining the scion to the root-stock with grafting tape, which holds the two pieces together until the graft has 'taken'. Nothing so easy for us, after all we were experimenting with nineteenth-century methods.

For joining the whip or tongue graft and keeping out the air and wet we had a choice of a number of old recipes. One was a wax seal which had to be applied warm. The recipe for it included pitch but was, according to the book we found it in, the 'least objectionable' of mixtures containing pitch. It consisted of eight pounds (3·6 kilograms) of resin, three pounds (1·3 kilograms) of tallow, three pounds (1·3 kilograms) of red ochre and one pound (0·45 kilogram) of burgundy pitch, all melted together in an iron pot. To keep the pot hot when it was taken off the fire it had to be kept on a hot brick, swopping the brick when it cooled for another hot brick. This sounded problematic, especially the constant supply of hot bricks.

93

There was an interesting cold wax recipe of melted resin, beef tallow and spirits of turpentine which had to be well corked, probably because of the seven ounces (200 cubic cm) of alcohol which had to be added. The alcohol cooled the mixture down considerably which meant it had to be put back on the heat. Unfortunately the alcohol had a tendency to catch fire. One way and another, wax seemed out. This left a clay mixture which, albeit a bit unsavoury, would suit our purposes. It was apparently particularly good for fruit trees as the clay retained moisture which helped the growing scion.

Mixing the concoction was not a job for the weak of stomach. A goodly dollop of clay had (preferably some weeks before it was required) to be kneaded to the consistency of soft soap. Just before making the graft, one part of fresh cow manure and one part of horse droppings had to be added. The cow manure mixed in well with the clay but the horse droppings remained obstinately insoluble. The problem was later tracked down to the fact that prior to mixing they should have been rubbed through a sieve. A good handful of finely-chopped hay was then mixed in to stop the mixture cracking.

How a scion and stock are prepared to achieve a graft is described quite succinctly by Mrs Loudon in her *Gardening for Ladies* (1840):

> Whip or Tongue grafting is where both the stock and the scion are cut in a slanting direction so as to fit each other, and a little slit is made in the stock into which a tongue or projecting part cut in the scion fits . . . as soon as the scion and the stock are properly fitted to each other, the parts are neatly bound together with a strand of bast steeped in water to make it flexible; and the bast is covered with a composition called grafting clay.

Mrs Loudon delicately omits to elaborate on the clay's composition.

There is a definite art to applying the clay. First, a small amount has to be rubbed over the bast or strips of matting used to bind the two pieces of wood together. This small amount has to be squeezed well in to seal all the crevices. Then a ball of clay has to be modelled round the join with the top and bottom end tapering so that the whole thing looks like a small melon or undersize rugby ball. As a final step it is necessary to have a basket of dry, finely sifted coal ashes nearby in which to plunge hands and render them appropriately coated enough to be able to press the clay into a perfect finish.

Clay sealing the graft

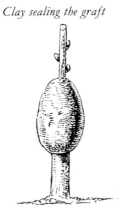

The embryo Maltster, complete with label, was left to take its chance in the nursery at Brogdale. There was hope of success as both scion and stock were of the same genus. Failure to recognise the need for stock and scion to be related must have caused some spectacular disappointments in days of antiquity. Classical scholars such as Aristotle and Pliny, either unaware of the necessary relation factor or hoping for miracles, wrote that vines could be grafted on to cherries, peach on to willow and that black roses would result from grafting a rose on to a blackcurrant bush.

Certainly by Victorian days fruit breeders were much more sophisticated and none more so than at the Rivers Nursery in Sawbridgeworth, Hertfordshire. It was accepted practice to graft pear scions on to quince stocks as this usually made the resultant pear tree a prolific bearer. There were some pear varieties such as Jargonelle and Marie Louise which were particularly choice but disappointingly 'shy' croppers. The remedy was obviously to graft them on to a quince stock to increase their fertility. Unfortunately, scions from these particular choice pear varieties would not 'take' to quince stock, any grafts attempted soon dying. In the 1850s nurseryman Thomas Rivers overcame this problem by offering as his speciality 'double-grafted' trees. Mr Rivers first grafted a pear variety which took readily to quince stock and then regrafted the graft on to the problem 'choice' varieties. In his own words there were 'many pears of the finest quality, but of a delicate and infertile habit' that could be much improved by double grafting.

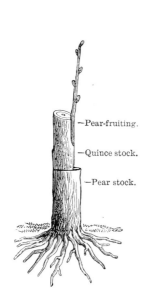

—Pear-fruiting.

—Quince stock.

—Pear stock.

Thomas Rivers' success with double grafting was only one of an extraordinary list of achievements. Today we rely on horticultural research stations to investigate the breeding and perfecting of new varieties, in Victorian times a handful of great nurserymen experimented, bred and imported new varieties. They relied on observation and their 'eye' for good stock. Of these nurserymen there is little doubt that Rivers was the most outstanding.

Thomas Rivers was born at Sawbridgeworth in Hertfordshire on 27 December 1798 into a family of nurserymen who had been trading since 1720. The nursery was a country one selling a mixture of cabbage plants, flowers and fruit trees with, interestingly, a glass of good currant wine to each customer.

Thomas Rivers was almost thirty when he succeeded his father in 1827. He was quick to see openings and rising trends. He noted that all standard rose trees were being imported from Paris and Rouen, providing a lucrative business for the French nurserymen. Rivers carried out some experiments to obtain his own standards. He eventually succeeded by budding roses on to the ready-made standards of the wild dog rose he found in the English woods and hedgerows. In 1833 he wrote his *Catalogue of Roses* which John Loudon, the famous horticultural encyclopaedist, called 'the most useful catalogue of roses in the English language'. Rivers followed this by publishing four years later *The Rose Amateur's Guide*, the first really practical work on the rose to appear in English.

From roses, Rivers turned his attention to fruit. In 1850 he wrote *The Miniature Fruit Garden*. The book ran to nineteen editions and it has been said that it revolutionised fruit gardening in England. When he was a youth looking around his father's nursery for good fruit to eat, Rivers had noticed that, surprisingly, the best fruit came not from the young, free-growing trees but from a group of 'refuse' trees. These trees had been considered too small or too weak for customers and had been designated to a piece of ground known as the hospital quarter. Rivers noted that these 'refuse' trees were taken up regularly and planted near together. He concluded that the annual disturbance kept the roots near to the ground surface, within the influence of sun and air, and that this was what kept the trees healthy and fruitful. In *The Miniature Fruit Garden* he urged readers to lift and prune regularly the roots of their fruit trees. This, he said, encouraged new root growth near the surface and would result in short, well-ripened fruit shoots.

Root pruning also kept in check the small pyramid-shaped fruit trees advocated by Rivers. He had visited the Continent several times and seen pyramidal trees being grown. He realised that small trees would be ideal for small gardens and for edging kitchen gardens. Small trees meant that less ground was lost to shade, a problem caused by the usual spreading standard tree. He experimented with dwarf root stocks and introduced Rivers Broad-leaved Paradise stock and Nonsuch Paradise. Fruit trees grafted on to these stocks, helped by root pruning, remained miniature enough to grow in the borders of the smallest gardens. By growing small trees, gardeners found that they could have more variety, and the other big bonus was that the trees could be easily protected to ensure a good supply of fruit.

In 1848 Thomas Rivers came up with the idea of 'orchard houses'. At his nursery he had small square spaces of ground enclosed by beech hedges which used to shelter delicate plants from cold winds and storms. Rivers covered one of the spaces with a piece of glass, using the beech hedges as supporting walls. Under the glass he made a turf bank to act as staging and sunk a pathway to give headroom. On the staging he grew, with great success, pots of peaches, nectarines and apricots. Ventilation percolated through the beech hedge and the only heat came from natural sunlight and the shelter the glass afforded. Encouraged by the success of this rough structure, he experimented with putting a glazed roof on to boarded sides, with ventilation openings back and front. This was even more successful. He then wrote a pamphlet called *The Orchard House* and gave the proceeds towards the restoration fund for Sawbridgeworth Parish Church. The pamphlet raised £189 and cleared the church repair debt completely. Eventually

Right: Pyramidal Morello cherry tree
Far right: Thomas Rivers
Below right: An orchard house of glass, wood and iron

it appeared as a book. A correspondent of the time wrote: 'The hold which the introduction of the orchard house took upon the gardening public was firm and rapid.' By the fifth edition of his book, Rivers was able to say: 'Orchard houses are now familiar things, hundreds are now rising up all over the face of the country; no garden structures have ever so rapidly advanced in popularity.'

The spread of the orchard house was no doubt helped, like the erection of greenhouses and forcing houses, by the removal of excise duty on glass. However, the orchard house differed from its companion glasshouses in that its purpose was to give superior protection to fruit trees which had formerly been grown on open walls and borders. The protection ensured the setting of the fruit in spring and the thorough ripening of wood during the autumn.

In summer, orchard houses could be difficult to keep cool. To combat this, Rivers invented an orchard-house railway. He built the central staging of the house on wheels. When required, the staging could run down two lines of rail laid through the house to an opening and take the trees with it for an *en masse* airing.

In the fourth edition of *The Orchard House*, Rivers wrote of constructing 'The Tropical Orchard House' and growing in it 'Mangosteen, Chirimoya, Pomegranate, Lee Chee, Loquat, Guava, Granadilla, Mango, Dwarf Plantain, Rose Apple, Sweet Lime, Sapodilla, Figs and Oranges. He also advocated orchard houses as sanatoriums, the dry air inside them being 'most agreeable in autumn, winter, and spring months for invalids'. He envisaged the day when in such dry and sunny counties as Surrey and Hampshire, orchard-house sanatoriums would abound and the fine air inside them be like the air of Nice but without its cutting wind.

By the sixteenth edition he was giving dimensions for 'Tropical Orchard Houses' with instructions about glazing, heating systems and hotbeds for the fruit pots. He particularly recommended a tangerine orange-house as a pleasant addition to the fruit garden and outlined plans for planting orange groves under glass to give perfumed promenades of fruit and flowers.

No one but an amateur of gardening can imagine the pure, quiet pleasure of taking a morning walk in the orange-house, full of aromatic flowers and fruit, during the dreary months of December and till the end of March, and plucking from the trees oranges fully ripe ... a large house – a real orange grove – would be a realisation of the gardens of the Hesperides.

Rivers himself specialised in oranges, growing over 3000 plants at his nursery. In 1876, when oranges which had been growing in California proved unsatisfactory, he sent out some of his trees from Sawbridgeworth. These trees included a variety called Valencia Late. So successful was this particular variety that it started the California orange-growing industry.

Following on the success of his orchard houses, Rivers invented a 'ground vinery'. As with root pruning, he attributed the germ of the idea back to his boyhood when he had wandered around the family nursery looking for the best fruit to eat. He found that in the vineyard planted by his grandfather, the largest and ripest bunches of grapes lay on the ground. In June 1860, Rivers studied a contrivance that was already on the market called the 'Curate's Vinery'. It was a ridge of glass placed over a furrow lined with slates. The bunches of grapes hung and ripened in the furrow. The great drawback to this invention was that when it rained the furrow filled with water. Thinking back to the grapes in his family vineyard, Rivers decided to build the Curate's Vinery on a new plan. On a piece of level ground he placed two rows of bricks endwise, leaving a gap between each brick for ventilation. Between the bricks he laid large tiles crosswise and on top of the bricks placed two seven-foot (2-metre) ridges of glass making a fourteen-foot-long (4-metre) vinery. He then planted a vine in the centre of the vinery and as it grew pegged it down through the spaces between the tiles. The heat of the sun was absorbed and radiated by the tiles and the grapes lying on the tiles ripened early and successfully.

One of the vines Rivers planted to test his new ground vinery was a Trentham Black. Five years later this vine was fifty feet (15 metres) long and bearing 130 bunches of grapes. It was said of the ground vinery that for 'the outlay of a few shillings on glass, any labourer or mechanic with a rod of ground could produce as good a dish of grapes as a peer'.

As well as inventing new garden structures, Thomas Rivers had extensive areas of fruit on trial, keeping careful records of his experiments. At one time he was growing over 1000 different varieties of pears but later rooted out several hundred which proved worthless.

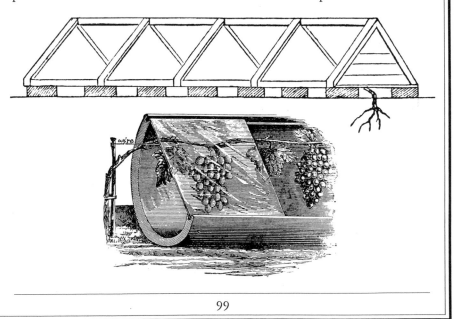

Rivers' Curate's Vinery and (below) a later commercial modification

An Early Rivers peach

The number he offered for sale at his nursery was however still considerable. He justified this by explaining that each variety differed in flavour; every grower has his particular favourites and some pear varieties adapted better to certain parts of the country than others. A visitor to the nursery reported seeing 6000 peach, nectarine and apricot trees in pots.

Rivers was particularly interested in prolonging the season of these fruits by raising early and late varieties. His success in breeding new varieties was remarkable. He succeeded in raising a peach which ripened far earlier than any other known. It was ripe on 4 July. He named it Early Beatrice in honour of Queen Victoria's youngest child. Then there was Early Louise ripening on 8 July, named to honour the

Princess Louise; and Early Rivers which ripened on 14 July. Early Victoria, Early Albert, Early Anne, Early Silver and an endless list of other successful peaches started their lives as Rivers' seedlings. Equally successful were late seedlings: The Prince of Wales, ripening in the middle of September; Lord Palmerston at the end of that month; Lady Palmerston at the beginning of October and many more, including all the varieties of both peach and nectarine which ripened mid-season. The extent of Rivers' prolific success can be gauged by thumbing through the pages which described peaches and nectarines in Hogg's *Fruit Manual*. The words *Raised by Mr Rivers of Sawbridgeworth* appear on practically every page of these sections.

Rivers used the old variety of nectarine Stanwick as part of the parenthood of many of his new varieties. The Stanwick was originally raised at Stanwick Park, the home of the Duke of Northumberland, from stones given by Her Majesty's Vice-Consul at Aleppo. The Duke of Northumberland gave the Stanwick Nectarine to Rivers to propagate and on 15 May 1850, twenty-four plants were sold by auction and realised £167 17s. od. which the Duke presented to the Gardeners' Benevolent Institution. It was an extraordinary amount of money for small pots of nectarine trees.

Although the Stanwick was well known for its superior flavour, it was apt to split easily when ripening. Rivers worked to raise peaches and nectarines which had the Stanwick flavour but not its habit of splitting. A gardening correspondent visiting the nursery in 1868 included the following in his report:

How very interesting it is to listen to Mr Rivers, while he is pulling fruit after fruit for one to taste, to hear him detailing the pedigree of each, with as much exactitude as is bestowed on some of our 'Derby Favourites'; to learn that this beautiful Peach we are now eating is a seedling, may be the 'third remove', as Mr Rivers terms it, from a yellow-fleshed Nectarine. Nectarines are raised from Peaches, and Peaches from Nectarines, without any sort of regularity.

In 1870 a memorial portrait of Thomas Rivers was commissioned to commemorate his services to horticulture. There were many subscribers towards the portrait; interestingly one of the names is Charles Darwin of Down in Beckenham. Rivers had corresponded with the author of *The Origin of Species* advising on fruit in Darwin's work on botany.

Thomas Rivers died in 1877. His son Thomas Francis Rivers succeeded him. He carried on his father's work at Sawbridgeworth, raising new varieties. Perhaps his most well-known introduction was the Conference pear, named at the time he was chairman of an International Fruit conference in 1888. Today, every fruit stall sells the popular Conference pear. There were several old Conference trees on the walls at Chilton which were pruned back to give them new life for our restoration project.

The fact that varieties of fruit bred by Thomas Francis Rivers' more famous father are still available a century or more after their introduction and recommended to us for planting at Chilton, was proof indeed of Thomas Rivers' skill as a horticulturalist. For the west-facing wall at Chilton we had planted fan-shaped Early Rivers cherries and for the south-facing wall a Lord Napier nectarine and a Rivers Early Prolific plum. Also bought and planted were fruits which Rivers had originally brought into Britain from France and America; Oullin's Golden Gage; Denniston's Superb plum and the apple American Mother. Robert Hogg dedicated the fifth edition of his classic *Fruit Manual* to the memory of Thomas Rivers. The first few words of the dedication seem particularly apt: 'Not that he requires a memorial other than that which he himself has raised . . .'

The descendants of Thomas Rivers carried on the business of nurserymen at Sawbridgeworth. After the First World War their main customers, the old houses with estate gardens, started to disappear. The business began to change, small gardens were not suited to fruit trees, exotic or otherwise. In 1985, after 265 years of trading, the Rivers Nursery finally and sadly closed down.

CHAPTER TEN

•

The value of cats and the Pest Remedy Finder —
Protecting fruit blossom —Bees and their surprising medicinal use.

Tuppence on patrol

THERE was a cat, Tuppence. He appeared from time to time from a door in one of the houses behind the garden bothy. On fine days he sat and washed himself on a patch of gravel between the house and a large tiled and red-brick building which had once been the estate dairy. The patch of gravel was the cat's territory but on some days, scratched and washed, he ventured for an exploratory sniff along the row of pots and potting sheds behind the north wall of the garden.

With the approach of March our speculative eyes fell on Tuppence's discreet ginger wanderings. Borders within the walled garden were ready for sowing. Also ready for the sowing was a colony of birds which lived in the hazel thicket around the fruit house. They reconnoitred daily on the north wall and swopped high-pitched notes on progress in the garden below. In addition to the hazel-grove harpies, a plump, bedraggled cock pheasant now regularly stalked the wall tops, gliding down to investigate and snaffle any tasty morsel which caught his eye.

It was time to take action, hence speculation over Tuppence's wanderings. 'For catching and deterring in a kitchen garden a good cat is worth its weight in silver,' the *Journal of Horticulture* had said in 1870.

Tuppence belonged to Ivy, who used to work in the dairy. Perhaps Ivy could persuade him to extend his perambulations to venture through the double wooden doors into the garden and conduct his grooming exercise on the path below the north wall. Given suitable encouragement, he might even patrol the rest of the garden. Bearing in mind his already ample diet, encouragements would have to be verbal rather than digestible. Had Tuppence been a true Victorian garden cat, his kitchen scrap ration would have been adequate enough to avoid his being tempted beyond the garden but not enough to be called over-feeding. By such careful balance, garden cats were ever alert and on patrol, keeping birds at a distance and mice out of sight.

Half-starving might sound harsh but garden cats were working animals. One old remedy to keep a border clear of vermin was to put a shelter at either end of the border, stretch a wire between the two shelters and attach a cat to the wire by means of a collar and chain around its neck.

Even kittens had their uses. In the *Cottage Gardener* for 1850 a correspondent explains how he kept birds away from his strawberries:

I have, at this time, a kitten tied with a string three-quarters of a yard long to a ring that slips on an iron rod placed horizontally; by this means the kitten can travel over a large space up and down, without having a long string to get entangled. It was thus treated as soon as it could eat and drink, and has not known what liberty is since; I have hung an empty cotton reel to a tree close by, which serves as a plaything, and the kitten appears to be 'as happy as the day is long'.

Semi-starving Tuppence or subjecting him to collars and chains – even with shelter in large flower pots – was not part of our plan. If such a scheme had been mentioned to Ivy, she would have scooped up Tuppence and slammed the garden door in our faces. It would be enough if Tuppence would deign to wander round the garden, especially just after sowing, and practise a baleful glare at any feathered spectators.

Apart from feline performance, we had to look at other forms of Victorian bird deterrents. These fell into two categories: those which could be tried and those which, although viewed as interesting, failed on humanitarian grounds, like the collar and chain. Into the first category fell pieces of looking-glass edged with strips of tin – the glass to flash in the sun and the tin to clatter in the breeze; seed protectors made from half-inch (1-cm) laths nailed together into a triangle shape with iron tacks nailed at the head of and down the sides of the triangle. Several of these needed to be made and placed at intervals either side of the seed bed with cotton or fine twine wound round the tacks and stretched across the bed like a web, triangle to triangle. A third deterrent was the good old-fashioned wind-propelled cherry clack.

A particularly nasty anti-bird device was a heavy stone supported by a peg and set with a forked twig. Corn was scattered under the stone, the bird flew on to the twig, moving it and displacing the peg which in turn brought the stone crashing down on top of the bird. Other nasties were lengths of stretched string tied with horsehair loops which turned into tightening nooses once birds became entangled and funnel-topped baskets which offered a tempting way in but no way out.

Birds were not the only predators we would have to deal with. Nineteenth-century remedies for mice, moles and insects were required reading before full-scale garden cultivation started. Harry had the old gardening books inherited from his head gardener uncle and there was a plentiful supply of other Victorian manuals, not to mention the odd remedy recommended in the *Journal of Horticulture* for the day or the *Cottage Gardener*. In fact it all became rather confusing because, after painstaking reading through several books, many of the old remedies and deterrents turned out to be the same but with different wording.

You could not, however, discard one book as being the same as another because every so often it would give a totally different remedy not appearing anywhere else.

To avoid further confusion, frayed pages and tempers, the simplest solution seemed to be to photocopy every pest remedy, discard the duplications and then paste up an at-a-glance Victorian Pest Remedy Finder which Harry could hang on his office door.

The final document, stretching from ants to woodlice, went roughly, with comments, as follows:

ANTS
(1) Place an inverted garden pot over nest and ants will work it. Remove pot in a day or two by placing spade beneath it. Plunge contents of pot into boiling water [*preferably find ants a new home*].
(2) Sprinkle sulphur under plant.
(3) Draw broad band of chalk along the wall and round stem of tree to keep ants away from ripening wall fruit.
(4) Stir up ants' nest, sprinkle with guano to drive them away [*difficult – guano no longer commercially available*].

APHIDS (or plant lice)
(1) Repeatedly syringe leaves and stem of plant with tobacco or lime water.
(2) Fumigate infected plant with tobacco, syringe afterwards with clear water, if not possible to fumigate wash with strong tobacco water applied with soft brush.
(3) Heat a plate of iron red-hot, then place quantity of true Cayenne pepper on it. Close (glass) house.
(4) Remove insects with aphis brush.
(5) Particularly for 'American Blight': brush trees with good stiff brush and a lather of soft soap in winter. If insects appear in spring rub paraffin freely into bark crevices with paintbrush.

Cherry clack

BIRDS
(1) Cats.
(2) Traps.
(3) Clacks.
(4) Stretched twine protectors.

BOYS
Smear garden wall top with red ochre and grease. Indelible mixture. Observe passing trouser seats.

CATERPILLARS

(1) To prevent on gooseberry bushes dust with hellebore powder or water with strong concoction of Digitalis or common foxglove. Both remedies deter sawfly laying eggs which lead to caterpillars.

(2) If caterpillars already present, sprinkle new lime under bushes, and fire a double-barrelled gun two or three times under bushes to shake caterpillars off into lime [*an interesting and dramatic remedy*].

(3) Remove top soil from under bushes and destroy grubs in it by mixing with salt or soot.

(4) Sprinkle lime or soot either over caterpillars or plants with an old flour dredger.

(5) Pick caterpillars off by hand.

(6) Encourage cuckoos into the garden. [*See 'The cuckoo is a great devourer of hairy caterpillars' article*, Journal of Horticulture, *10 June 1875.*]

CRICKETS

Put a common white glazed jar nine or ten inches high in place they infest. Drop a slice or two of cucumber into it plus one live cricket as a decoy. Crickets will hop in but be unable to hop out. When jar is one-third full fill with boiling water [*find crickets a new home*].

EARWIGS

(1) Place pieces of hollow stem four to six inches long in a horizontal position in different parts of tree. Earwigs will congregate in these and can be shaken out into boiling water [*find a new home*].

(2) Place pieces of linen rags in clusters in lower parts of tree – earwigs take refuge in these at certain times of day. Note times and dispose of linen rags accordingly.

(3) Old shoes with wisps of hay in them placed at bottom of tree or 'thumb pots' filled with hay and placed sideways in large forks of tree or at base.

(4) Patent Earwig traps.

MEALY BUGS

Wash with dilution of methylated spirits or paraffin.

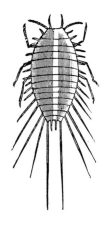

MICE (including house-mouse, field-mouse, short- and long-tailed mouse)

(1) To prevent mice eating newly sown peas and beans and flower bulbs – saturate beforehand with solution of bitter aloes or soak in salad oil and roll in powdered resin. Place chopped furze in drills where seeds sown.

Left (from top): Cater-
pillars, earwig, earwig
trap and mealy bug
Right: Mouse traps
Below: Belgian Mole Trap
Below right: Onion fly,
larva and chrysalis

(2) Mouse traps:

(i) Common mouse traps – smear wires with grease to prevent rusting.

(ii) Pickle jar sunk to brim in ground. Smear rim and inside of jar with grease half filled with water. Place corn or cheese near jar. Mice come for bait, slip over rim and drown in submerged pickle jar.

A variation on above:

Sunken glazed pot with a pronged wheel rotating on a stick placed across pot. Bait fixed on pronged wheel which rotates as mouse tries to eat. Mouse slips into water in pot.

MOLES

(1) Place green leaves of common elder into their tunnels – smell offensive to them.

(2) Set fire to a paraffin-soaked rag in the opening of the run.

(3) Watch for them between the hours of 9 am and 3 pm (hillock-making time). Eject with a fork [*optimistic and time-consuming*].

(4) Mole traps:

(i) Bucket sunk beneath ground on a level with floor of the run. Flat piece of board laid over the run, earth heaped on it to exclude light.

(ii) The Belgian Mole Trap. Gruesome spiked block. Viewed as humane as causes death instantaneously [*barbaric! Included for interest only*].

ONION FLY

Sprinkle gas lime on earth between rows of onions.

RABBITS
(1) Place boards connected with hooks and eyes (for ease of removal) round stems and trunks.
(2) Sticks placed round tree and bound with tarred cord.

RED SPIDER
(1) $\frac{1}{2}$ lb tobacco, $\frac{1}{2}$ lb sulphur, $\frac{1}{2}$ peck lime
Stir well in three or four gallons of water. Leave to settle then syringe trees and walls.
(2) Soft soap, sulphur and clay beaten up to consistency of paint with warm water.
(3) Fumigation by putting sulphur on to hot plates.

SCALE
Destroy by the application of strong soapy water in the proportion of 1 oz of soap to 1 quart of water, paraffin in the proportion of $\frac{1}{4}$ gill to 1 gallon, lye of wood ashes or potash, tobacco water and fish oil.

SLUGS
To destroy small white and black garden slugs:
(1) Put fresh powdered lime into a coarse bag. After nightfall or at sunrise dust the ground where slugs are.
(2) Strew fresh cabbage leaves on ground in evening. Slugs hide under them during night – collect slugs in morning [*preferably find them new home*].

Below: Thrips and a wasp trap

SNAILS
(1) Pick off by hand into bucket.
(2) Make thick paste of train oil and soot and daub on bottom of wall – snails will not attempt to pass it.

THRIPS
Tobacco water or strong soap water.

WASPS
(1) Hang bottles containing sugar and beer dregs in the tree.
(2) Find wasps' nest. In evening rinse a common wine bottle well with spirits of turpentine, while bottle still wet thrust neck into main entrance of nest stopping up other holes. Fumes of turpentine stupefy then destroy wasps. Wait a few days then dig up nest.
(3) Leave wasp-damaged fruits on tree. When fresh wasps re-attack fruit cut them in two with grape scissors [*dangerous and nasty*].

WOODLICE

Destroy by pouring boiling water on to them [*there must be another solution somewhere?*].

One anti-mouse remedy had already been tried. Before planting peas, Harry had first soaked them in paraffin then rolled them around an old tin which had a layer of red lead in the bottom. Wearing gloves, as the red lead was poisonous, he dropped the coated peas into the soil then, as a further deterrent, placed a dressing of chopped gorse on top. Apparently mice have an uncanny knack of finding newly-sown peas but Harry thought that any mouse would think twice before rubbing its nose into the prickly gorse. It worked. Unmolested by so much as a mouse's whisker, the pea shoots appeared green and strong.

The red spider eggs which lodged like heaps of orange fly spots in the crevices of the peach trees were also in for a shock. Harry assembled a container of what, apart from its colour, looked like ladies' cleansing cream. It was brown and smelt of kippers. He also had a half-pound (227 grams) bag of yellow sulphur and a tin of white tobacco powder which, despite bearing the pre-war price of 1s. 6d. (8p), was still full. When the lid was prised off, the contents caught the back of the throat like a bulldog. For mixing there was a yellow glazed bowl with the word POISON dimly printed into the base, and a watering can full of hot water.

Tebb's Universal Fumigator

The kippery cleansing cream turned out to be soft soap, a generous handful of it was scooped out and plopped into the bowl, followed by a heavy sprinkling of sulphur and a pinch or two of tobacco powder. Harry kneaded the three together then, taking up a handful of the mixture, dusted it with more sulphur from the packet and moulded first one, then three, perfect dumplings which he set neatly beside the mixing bowl. The empty bowl was pushed to one side and the dumplings transferred into the bottom of a bucket and subjected to a stream of hot water from the watering can until the bucket was one-third full. With a makeshift wooden batten Harry swirled the rapidly dissolving dumplings until the bucket frothed into noxious yellow scum. Then, taking an old stubby paintbrush, all the better for getting into crevices, he took both bucket and brush to begin a combined baptism and last rites for the red spider. Left unanointed the eggs would have hatched out and the minute red spiders caused the leaves on the peach tree to wither and die and the branches to be fruitless.

Loss of fruit from insect damage was one hazard but come March and early April there was another threat to the productivity of the walled fruit trees. Cold winds and snap frosts could shrivel the blossom and render the trees barren, particularly the tender, more exotic species. The apricots, peaches and nectarines planted against the south-facing wall at Chilton might well have to be protected.

There were a number of methods of protecting blossom from frost. One of the oldest was to use cuttings of small branches of laurel, yew or fir, pushing the evergreens between the branches of the fruit tree and spreading out their leaves to cover the blossom. This had to be done just as the trees were coming into blossom and the evergreens – or if they were unavailable, dried ferns – left in place until the fruit was set and as big as large peas.

Another method was to cover the trees with straw screens which during the day could be taken down and rolled up. Once fixed in place the screens were, according to an account in 1856, capable of protecting the trees from the effects of 12 degrees Fahrenheit of frost. Their efficiency was put down to the fact that the straws, being hollow, contained air and this made them good insulators.

Equally removable were large canvas mats fastened at one end with nails and hooks to the top of the wall and left to hang down over the trees. The bottoms had to be fastened down to stop them beating against the blossom. In mild weather the mats could be unhooked.

Canvas could also be hung from a temporary coping which projected eighteen inches (46 cm) or so from the top of the wall. A popular canvas was called 'Frigi Domo'. It was made of prepared hair and wool and was advertised as keeping a fixed temperature wherever it was applied. In addition to frost protection, its manufacturers claimed it to be equally effective against sun, winds and insects, and claimed as their patrons, Her Majesty the Queen, the Duke of Devonshire and Sir Joseph Paxton.

A far prettier covering than matting was being explored in 1862 by a Mr Gorrie. The *Book of Garden Management* related Mr Gorrie's plans to train an Ayrshire Rose on a trellis under a projecting coping. This particular variety of rose was thought to be admirably suited for the purpose as it grew rapidly in spring.

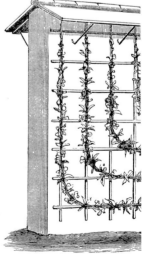

The Reverend John Lawrence also had a variation on the traditional. Instead of one overhead coping, he fastened on to the side of his garden wall thin pieces of board and tile in descending horizontal lines. The tiles overhung the lateral branches of each fruit tree with gaps every so often to accommodate the upright tree trunk and branches.

Even in the most difficult year a good quantity of fruit may almost be depended upon from such blossoms as are sheltered by the tiles. The fruit thus sheltered from perpendicular cold and blasts I have experienced to be much larger, better, and finer-tasting, than those of the same tree where exposed.

Overhead board coping gave way to glass set on ornamental iron brackets which were bolted into the upper part of the wall and connected by purlins on which the glass rested. Thick panes were less susceptible to weather damage.

These glass copings could project as far as three feet (1 metre) from the wall and sometimes had glass sashes fixed against them. The sashes sloped down to the ground and fitted into grooves so that they could be opened by sliding behind or in front of each other, or in the summer removed altogether. Sometimes the glass in the overhead coping was constructed so that it, too, could be removed. This was useful in summer to allow rain on to the leaves and young fruit and if the panes were removed in winter it helped to keep the trees cool and dormant.

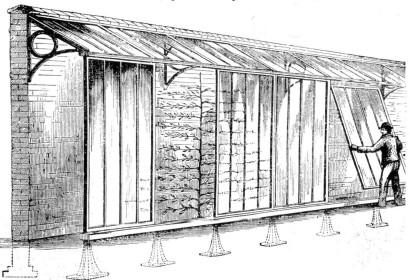

By the 1870s the sophistication of glazed shelter for walled fruit was being reflected in trade names. One particular style was known as 'The Crymoboethus' (the literal interpretation apparently means a good protector from frost). This not only protected the walled fruit but was also sufficiently roomy to offer shelter to plants and seedlings.

The walls beneath glazed fruit protectors were whitened to compensate for any light lost by the overhead glazing. In today's neglected kitchen gardens, where plots and borders merge into one wilderness and sheds and houses have long since disappeared, more often than not these ephemeral glass structures can still be traced. Rusting coping brackets, still firmly bolted, some intact, some broken, jut out over whitewashed walls supporting pure fresh air, their glass as vanished as the delicate trees they once protected. Chilton had no evidence of glass copings. Possibly none were ever built, the inside fruit houses providing sufficient peaches and nectarines, and perhaps matting was used around the outside trees. Not far from Chilton there is, however, an extraordinary sight which Harry Dodson recommended my seeing. On a large country estate there is a walled kitchen garden still partially cultivated – although no longer to the extent that it was in its heyday. Running the entire length of 105 feet (32 metres) of the east wall of this garden is a glass coping roof, brackets and panes all totally intact, and beneath it, trained pear trees. In spring, the blossoms beneath the glass are a sight to behold. As the year progresses and the pears ripen, the coping gives another bonus. Old hooks running along its outer edge provide convenient hanging points for curtains of tiffany or netting. The falling material screens the trees against marauding birds and wasps and possibly against bees too, although honey bees (if our source in the *Journal of Horticulture* for 1871, 'Bees Not Fruit Robbers', was to be believed) never attack sound fruit. Apparently these striped gentlemen of the air resist temptation even when 'presented' with fresh fruit, and are content with 'fruit in a half-decomposed state'.

Assured by this and our source's further remarkable findings that 'a smart bee-sting or two' in hot, sultry weather benefited gardeners by causing them to 'perspire more freely, and feel much lighter afterwards', we gratefully accepted the offer of an antique beehive for Chilton. The hive, built in about 1875, was not, as we had imagined, a straw skep. It turned out to be a handsome, heavy, wooden structure – the battens on the underside of its eight-panelled roof as complex as the rafters of a cathedral. A few of these battens had seen better days and a clumsy past repair made one corner of the roof more prominent than its fellows. In return for sympathetically restoring the hive we were given it on loan, complete with bees. This was a pleasing state of affairs, for any benefits to perspiration flow would have been outweighed by the ill-luck apparently brought by bees if you actually pay money for them!

The bees needed a temperature of 54 degrees Fahrenheit (12°C) before becoming resident. They were brought in early May and their refurbished home set in the sheltered south-west corner of the garden – a short bee-line from the cut flower border.

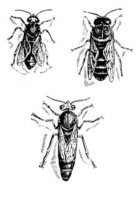

Above: Worker, drone and queen bee
Left: New beehives of the 'most approved kinds', advertised in Cottage Gardener, 1852

CHAPTER ELEVEN

•

Great Gooseberry Shows – Strawberries and the disappearance
of a silver cup – Retarding currants.

BUSH and berried fruit in the garden were beginning to burgeon by early summer, although it had been touch and go with the gooseberries – not in their cultivation but in actually obtaining them in the first place.

For the bushes to look attractive in the relatively short time allowed for the restoration project, we needed to have ones which had been trained at the nursery into double cordons – a large wishbone shape. Wires had been fixed along the edges of the main vegetable plots to enable cordons to continue growing. This method of using gooseberry cordons as an edging to vegetable plots was greatly favoured by some head gardeners. William Crump, head gardener at Madresfield Court, had treble cordons and, more unusually, quadruple cordons planted eighteen inches (46 cm) apart, each gooseberry bush with four stems trained up in pairs to a height of six feet (2 metres).

Unlike Brussels sprouts and strawberries, there was no problem in finding Victorian varieties. One gooseberry specialist was still growing over fifty nineteenth-century species. We had decided on six each of: Early Sulphur, London, Broom Girl, Lancashire Lad, Keepsake and Careless. The varieties were chosen for their flavour, colour and historical interest.

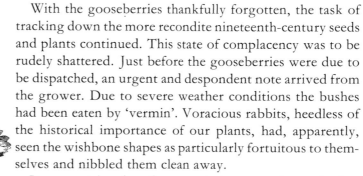

With the gooseberries thankfully forgotten, the task of tracking down the more recondite nineteenth-century seeds and plants continued. This state of complacency was to be rudely shattered. Just before the gooseberries were due to be dispatched, an urgent and despondent note arrived from the grower. Due to severe weather conditions the bushes had been eaten by 'vermin'. Voracious rabbits, heedless of the historical importance of our plants, had, apparently, seen the wishbone shapes as particularly fortuitous to themselves and nibbled them clean away.

It was getting late for re-ordering gooseberry bushes and anxious calls to a number of nurseries revealed that stocks had been sold and there were no old-type double cordons to be had anywhere – well, almost anywhere. One splendid grower in Wakefield, Yorkshire, went out into the bitter weather to check his stocks and thought that he could supply the order. He had no bushes which were actually trained as double cordons but he would choose ones which had the sort of growth that Harry could train into shape. This was an extreme relief. Not to have gooseberries in a Victorian garden would have been an insult to a fruit which came to glory at that time.

Gooseberries were certainly being grown in gardens by Elizabethan times. They were not seen as luxury fruits but were cooked small and green. By 1629 John Parkinson wrote in *Paradisi in Sole, Paradisus Terrestris*: 'Wee have divers sorts of Gooseberries, besides the common kinde, which is of three sorts, small, great, and long. For wee have three red Gooseberries, a blew and a greene.' The last mentioned berries were not so tart as the ordinary gooseberry and were 'eaten at pleasure' instead of being cooked.

The extraordinary story of British interest in gooseberry breeding (which resulted in Robert Hogg in his *Fruit Manual* being able to list 225 different varieties – red, yellow, green, white, round, oblong, oval, obovate, smooth, downy, rough or hairy) is worth telling.

In Lancashire, the Midlands and Cheshire in the second half of the eighteenth century an interest sprang up amongst handloom weavers in breeding what were known as florist flowers. This interest in cross-breeding and exhibiting also extended to gooseberries, which did well in the moist climate of these areas.

It was not so much the colour or the flavour which gradually began to obsess growers but the size and weight of the berry. Shows were held at which berries were weighed individually on apothecary's scales using weights of pennyweights and grains. The Gooseberry Growers' Register, published annually, listed names and weights of prize berries. The earliest copy of the register dates from 1786.

Competition was keen. To encourage monstrous berries, Lancashire exhibitors picked most of the berries from each bush and 'suckled' the remaining individual berries by placing a pan of water under each in the hope that the berry would swell out with the vapour given off by the water. Planting of new bushes was also a careful process. The intended site was dug and filled with a mixture of rich topsoil and well-rotted manure, more mulching was done when the bush was planted and it was then supplied with liquid manure to encourage growth.

As the days approaching the shows began, heavy rain was dreaded. This could cause the berries to burst. There is a story that a Middleton silk weaver woke one night to hear the beginnings of a thunderstorm. He leapt out of bed and carried his quilt downstairs to protect his gooseberry bushes from the rain. The shows were held in local inns and copper kettles, pans and teapots were awarded to the winners: the owners of the heaviest berries. The success of selecting and cosseting gooseberries reached a dizzy height in 1852. In that year in Staffordshire the purplish-red gooseberry variety called London weighed in at thirty-seven pennyweights and seven grains (58 grams). A measure of this achievement can be gauged by comparing this with the weight of the wild gooseberry – a puny five pennyweights (8 grams). The London holds the daunting record of having been the heaviest berry for thirty-eight seasons, from 1829 to 1867. It is celebrated in the Gooseberry Growers' Song, sung to the tune of 'With Wellington, we'll go, we'll go':

Come all ye jovial gardeners, and listen unto me,
Whilst I relate the different sorts of winning gooseberries,
This famous institution was founded long ago,
That men might meet, and drink, and have a gooseberry show.

CHORUS
So come all jovial gardeners, let's merry, merry be:
We'll sing and dance, we've all a chance, but the London is for me.

This London of renown, was that famous Huntsman's son,
Who was raised in a Cheshire village near the May-pole in Acton,
While in bloom he was but small, yet still so fast he grew,
That everyone admired him, for his equals are but few.

The rest of the song, now known as the Gooseberry Growers' Anthem, describes the challenge thrown out by the gooseberry variety Lion to the London, the Lion's defeat and an intriguing list of other names:

There's Dan's Mistake and Catherina, Magenta and Careless too,
Clayton, Drill and Telegraph, Antagonist and Peru;
Mount Pleasant, Plunder, King of Trumps, Australia and Railway,
Ploughboy, High Sheriff and Gretna Green; but the Bobby wins the day.

... and so it goes on, filling another five verses with other names as diverse as Macaroni and Queen Victoria. Naming was evidently a personal thing, with beauty very much in the eye of the beholder. Two growers bred berries which turned out hairy and creamy white – one called his Jenny Lind, the other Weasel.

In addition to the shows, local inns were also the venue for 'letting out' berries. This was the way in which new varieties became established. The gooseberry grower had to have a berry which had won a prize and which satisfied judges that there was not another like it. The mother plant was then cut up into twenty-one lots and each piece sold off and even that was not the end of it. Judges stipulated that in two years, berries from the 'let-outs' should be brought back and weighed, just to make sure the original had not been a one-off.

The gooseberry Dan's Mistake owes its name to the fact that a grower seems to have mixed up an odd piece in amongst his twenty-one cuttings. This odd piece grew red berries whilst the others grew yellow. The red-berried one proved to be a winner and became known as 'Dan's Mistake'. Other mistakes were not so happy. One grower let out a berry which was found to be almost identical to the already existing Roaring Lion and, by way of compensation, had to give three different varieties to each person who had bought from him.

One variety closely resembling another can prove confusing, and sorting out the confusion has become a way of life for Dave Smith of Bolton. He is attempting to put a name to each of the 220 gooseberry bushes forming the National Gooseberry Collection, which are planted near the Jodrell Bank radio-telescope. Mr Smith spends long hours in libraries, takes berries home to assess their colour, shape and texture, sends abroad for extracts on gooseberries in foreign reference books and spends time looking in old gardens, all in an attempt to put the right name on the appropriate gooseberry. It is not an easy task when you consider the vast number of gooseberries bred and the variety names. There are any number of Red Champions and Green Champions and Whites, which are only white depending on the way you look at them. The work is a labour of love to Mr Smith. After all, he says, where else would you find Lloyd George, Thatcher and George Brown all in the same bed?

In addition to copper kettles, many of which have been passed down to descendants, Victorian gooseberry growers could win a variety of other prizes. A certain Benjamin Butterworth won an impressive list of articles which included a pig, a ham, a metal teapot, a rocking chair and seven sets of china. The same interesting generality exists today. Mr George Hulme has a radio, a clock and various other prizes won at the annual Goostrey Gooseberry Show.

Goostrey is one of eight Gooseberry Clubs which today form the Mid-Cheshire Gooseberry Shows Association. Around the end of July, tension rises with the approach of show days. Three of the Association's shows are held on one day: Goostrey, Lower Peover and Holmes Chapel. The Goostrey show is held in the school hall, the Lower Peover show at the Crown and the Holmes Chapel show at the Red Lion. Despite their close proximity, it takes stamina to attend all three.

The night before the show, the polythene covering the gooseberry cages is pulled back (or in the case of Mr Cragg from Lower Peover, the brightly-coloured golfing umbrellas removed), and the chosen berries are picked. Traditionally, this is done in the presence of witnesses. The grower weighs the berries on his own scales to form an idea of their potential, then carefully places them in a specially-built wooden box. Still in front of witnesses, the wooden box is tied down and a blob of hot sealing wax dropped on to the knot. Veteran boxes are decorated with singes and crusts of past seals. The boxes will not be opened until the commencement of the show on the following afternoon. A certain amount of anxiety follows the sealing down. It has been known for 'dead certs' to burst in the box overnight and there is speculative talk about competitors suddenly being attacked by sneezes as they open their boxes and having to bring their handkerchiefs into play. Bursting has also been the bitter experience of growers who leave their best berry on the bush for a few more days for a later show.

In the pubs or hall, competitors and boxes form a horseshoe at the top of which the officials sit with a pair of apothecary's scales and the required pennyweights and grains. It is a serious business and some box tops remain mere slits as men (not many women appear to take part, it seems) slide their hands under the lids to produce contenders.

Gooseberry grower sizing up his chances on show day

The most important prize is for the Premier Berry. This is the heaviest of any kind or colour. Those who think they may be lucky offer their berry to an official who takes it to the top table to be weighed. However, another contender berry put into the other dish of the scales may outweigh it. This continues until one berry proves unbeatable and is officially weighed with the pennyweights and grains. This Premier Berry is then given a place of honour on a large display board which faces the assembly and which, by the end of the tense afternoon, will be glistening with berries, many the size of large bantam eggs. Following the Premier, there are Triplets (three berries grown on one stalk) .and then Twins (two on a stalk). These sometimes cause a predicament for the grower. Should a particularly good twin have been split so that one of them could have been entered for the Premier Berry? Then follow awards for the best colours – red, yellow, green and white – and awards for the best maiden grower and the Best Beaten Berry. These twentieth-century shows follow the tradition of Victorian days and help to explain why so many different varieties of gooseberry appeared in the patrician confines of the walled kitchen garden.

Another berry which seems to have always tickled aristocratic taste-buds but which also reached an important stage of development in Victorian times is the strawberry.

Of the hundred or more varieties available during the last half of the nineteenth century only one variety still remains, Royal Sovereign. This strawberry scrapes in as Victorian by virtue of the fact that it was introduced in 1892. Every other old variety has succumbed to virus disease. Even Royal Sovereign was not easy to find. As soon as the crowns became established on their bed laid across the sunny top half of the main vegetable plot, Harry started to augment the supply. As each plant threw out straggly runners he placed a stone on every runner, pressing it against the soil and encouraging it to put out roots. Eventually we ended up with over double the original number.

Royal Sovereign was bred by Thomas Laxton, the last of a distinguished line of Victorian strawberry breeders. The first large-fruited variety of strawberry, the forefather of the type we buy today, was bred in 1821 by Michael Keens, a market gardener of Isleworth in Middlesex. He called it Keens' Seedling. Part of its parentage was the *Fragaria chilensis*, or Chilean Strawberry, the largest species of wild strawberry. The biggest berries from Keens' Seedling measured two inches (5 cm) in diameter at their widest and an inch and a half (3·8 cm) in depth. Edward Bunyard, author of *Handbook of Hardy Fruits*, writes:

Fragaria chilensis

The large size and excellent flavour of this fruit created a sensation which probably no succeeding strawberry has ever equalled. The Royal Horticultural Society showed its approval by a coloured plate in its *Transactions* (Vol. V p.261) and presenting the raiser with a silver cup. It is interesting to note that this cup exists in London at the present time.

Interesting indeed! Bunyard was writing in the 1920s. Was this silver cup, of such importance in the history of the strawberry, still available to public eyes? A call to the Royal Horticultural Society sent them looking up the reference and then searching in the basement. Not a glint of the cup was there. The coloured plate in the *Transactions* was certainly to hand but they could not find any record of that time saying that Keens had been awarded a silver cup. How odd. Further foraging in their limitless horticultural tomes produced an article by Charles Curtis which had appeared in the *Gardeners' Chronicle* in 1950. Writing of Micheal Keens, Mr Curtis said that Keens had a friend and neighbour called John Wilmot who was also a raiser of strawberries and who lived at Isleworth. Mr Wilmot's market gardens were subsequently taken over by a Mr Joseph Taylor. Mr Taylor had been a friend of Charles Curtis and when Mr Taylor died Curtis inherited a silver cup which had stood on Mr Taylor's sideboard. In Mr Curtis' words:

It is of no great monetary value: five-and-a-quarter-inches high, with a diameter of three inches at the mouth and of deep wineglass form; but the inscription reads: 'Presented by the Hampshire Horticultural Society to Mr Michael Keens, for his production of an excellent Seedling Strawberry at their Meeting in June, 1830'.

Charles Curtis died eight years after writing the article. What happened to either of these silver cups is still not known.

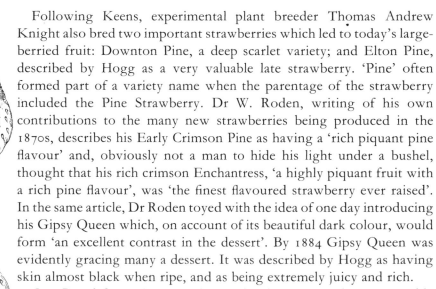

Following Keens, experimental plant breeder Thomas Andrew Knight also bred two important strawberries which led to today's large-berried fruit: Downton Pine, a deep scarlet variety; and Elton Pine, described by Hogg as a very valuable late strawberry. 'Pine' often formed part of a variety name when the parentage of the strawberry included the Pine Strawberry. Dr W. Roden, writing of his own contributions to the many new strawberries being produced in the 1870s, describes his Early Crimson Pine as having a 'rich piquant pine flavour' and, obviously not a man to hide his light under a bushel, thought that his rich crimson Enchantress, 'a highly piquant fruit with a rich pine flavour', was 'the finest flavoured strawberry ever raised'. In the same article, Dr Roden toyed with the idea of one day introducing his Gipsy Queen which, on account of its beautiful dark colour, would form 'an excellent contrast in the dessert'. By 1884 Gipsy Queen was evidently gracing many a dessert. It was described by Hogg as having skin almost black when ripe, and as being extremely juicy and rich.

Our Royal Sovereign was the result of a crossing between Noble and King of the Earlies. Most Victorian strawberry names seem to have a certain grandeur, there being an assortment of Queens, Princes, Comtes, Empresses and Princesses. Hairy Red, Shiner, Thumper and Weasel in the gooseberry lists might have sounded a mite more mundane, but a Strawberry Growers' Song based on the lines of the Gooseberry Growers' Anthem would hardly have sent feet tapping.

At Chilton it was thought at first that it might be a good idea to follow the advice given in the *Book of Garden Management* of 1862 and place tiles under the best strawberries to accelerate their ripening. (Apparently in some establishments, where expense was no object, tiles were cut so as to join round the roots of the plant and fit together.) Mr Cuthill's views in Delamer's *Kitchen Garden* put paid to this notion. Mr Cuthill, who was evidently an authority, believed that tiles harboured insects and the hot sun reflecting on them ripened the berries prematurely making them still acid when picked. Tiles under berries were acceptable for market strawberries but definitely not for private gardens.

Several packets of Alpine strawberries had resulted in sufficient plants to fill two small borders alongside the melon and cucumber house. These small strawberries resembled sweet British wild strawberries, except that their shape was pointed, not round. Alpine strawberry plants were popular as edging to borders, their small fruit being favoured by Victorians for use in fruit salads. It was also said that preserving them in sugar brought out their peculiar aromatic flavour. The Alpines would bear in summer and again in early autumn.

Like strawberries, raspberries had one solitary survivor from the last

Above (from top): Early Crimson Pine, Enchantress and Gipsy Queen

century: fine, mild, sweet-flavoured but, alas, prone to virus, the Yellow Antwerp. Introduced into this country from Belgium by a Mr North of Lambeth, the Yellow Antwerp was now grown by only one nursery, at Wimbotsham in Norfolk. Three dozen canes arrived at Chilton and, under Harry's care, were growing, slender, pale companions beside the vulgarly healthy twentieth-century red Glen Clova.

Above: Raspberries
Below: Currants

Trained against wires along the top of the main left-hand vegetable plot, fifteen cordons of both red and white currants showed every indication of bearing well. The white started to gleam, translucent like mistletoe berries. They were White Dutch, one of a couple of nine-teenth-century white varieties still being sold. White currants were considered less acid than red and preferred for the Victorian dining-table. Sometimes they were mixed with red for contrast in desserts. Our Red Dutch berries would have been prepared in the kitchens as a preserve for pies, tarts and jellies or set aside to make wine. In more recent times, Harry remembers growing red currants to be sent up to the house kitchens which were then dipped in Cointreau, rolled in icing sugar and hung to dry before being served at table.

Less favoured by our ancestors was the blackcurrant. It was thought to have an unpleasant, medicinal taste, although blackcurrant wine was said to be sweeter than that from red, particularly when it was served warm and spiced. *Kettner's Book of the Table* published in 1877 considered that 'the blackcurrant has little to do with cookery, except as the faithful attendant of Roly Poly'. The blackcurrant only became acceptable as dessert with the introduction of a variety called Black Naples. This had larger berries and a milder, sweeter flavour than previous varieties. Black Naples is no longer available but one of today's varieties, Baldwin, is thought by many fruit experts to be Black Naples by another name. Eventually thirty purchased two-year-old Baldwins were making abun-dant growth in a line beside the raspberries.

There was an old method of making sure that both currants and gooseberries could be supplied to the dining-room for as long a period of time as possible. Known as 'retarding', this involved putting mats over the ripening berries the moment they changed colour. The *Cottage Gardener* for 1850 recommended carrying out the practice in two stages: first by covering one half of the bushes immediately and then covering the remaining portion two weeks later. The berries covered early had to have their covering removed every week for a day or two so that they acquired colour and flavour at a slow pace. Although not so highly flavoured as those covered when they were mature, this slow ripening method ensured berries which would keep for far longer and enable the gardener to offer a choice of dessert fruits into the autumn.

CHAPTER TWELVE

•

Pineapples and the trials of growing them – Vines large and small,
including the usefulness of grape bottles and a social dilemma.

ULTIVATING pineapples at Chilton, as they would have
been in the last century, was an impossible task. Lack of
adequate heating and time were both against us. A growing
pineapple was given a constant heat of 80 degrees Fahrenheit (27°C) in
summer and 70 degrees (21°C) in winter and could take up to eighteen
months to fruit. But for the sake of bringing back this 'King of the
Fruits' which held the highest position on the Victorian dining-table,
it was agreed that even the impossible should be attempted.

Harry thought the first thing to do to reduce the time problem was
to get hold of some 'fruiting maidens'. These are plants already started
which, after a few months, would bear pineapples from a single stalk
rising from the centre of the leaves. He might as well have asked for
gold-plated plants, they would have been as easy to find. Not one
nursery or botanical garden in Britain had available a pineapple plant
in any shape or form, let alone a supply of fruiting maidens.

Perhaps this should not have been too surprising weighed against
the information given to us by Horace Parsons, now sadly deceased,
who was at one time head gardener to the Queen at Sandringham. He
had told us that in 1914 all the pine 'stoves' in private gardens closed
down. Mr Parsons' employer at the time had been car magnate Lord
Rootes. Lord Rootes insisted that, despite others' wartime economies,
his pineapple stoves be kept in production. This put Mr Parsons in the
unique position for some years afterwards of being the only gardener
in the country growing pineapples in the old way.

The dodo-like demise of British-grown pineapples meant assistance
would have to be sought from overseas. Through the kind and puzzled
help of this country's largest pineapple importer, arrangements were
made for a quantity of fruiting maidens to be dispatched from one of
their South African pineries. It was not at all as straightforward as it
sounded. Permission had to be sought from the Ministry of Agriculture,
who had to consider the request before granting an import licence. A
licence was dependent upon a phytosanitary certificate being supplied
from South Africa which in turn was dependent on the plants having
been inspected by the local plant health officer and cleared of bugs and

disease. It was also necessary to undertake that the plants be sent free of all soil and inspected immediately on their arrival at London Airport.

The stringency of all these administrative regulations was blown by a single and embarrassing phone call. Four cardboard boxes were sitting under a desk in Borough Market, London – could they be collected please? Innocent of and unattended by phytosanitary certificate or any other official blessing, the boxes contained twenty-four pineapple plants in various stages of exhaustion. A well-meaning South African plantation worker had, as an afterthought, thrust them aboard with a consignment of fruit bound for London. The Ministry of Agriculture was understandably horrified at the news. It seemed that, in addition to exhaustion, the plants would have to suffer instant cremation. A series of frantic phone calls and solemn undertakings ensued. Provided that the boxes remained unopened, were immediately taken to Long Ashton (a plant research station near Bristol), incarcerated in an insect-proofed glass case, certified as pest-free by a Ministry inspector *and* kept in quarantine for as long as required, then they could live.

It was an alarming and inauspicious start to our pineapple project. The pines in their white glass case looked sick, not through disease but merely through lack of proper carriage and water. The Ministry inspector passed them as free from foreign bugs but the kind, white-coated technicians at Long Ashton shook their heads over the brown and withering appendages that had once started life as leaves. There was no alternative, the plants would have to remain in intensive care. It was Christmas time, seven months later, before they were allowed to be moved to Chilton. There they were positioned in an old glass-house, the pots plunged deep into beds of fermented beech-leaves. Miraculously, and helped by their stay at Long Ashton, some fruited.

To us the archaic sight of a house of growing pineapples was as extraordinary as the first pineapple to enter the country must have seemed to Oliver Cromwell, who received a fruit from ambassadors returning from China in 1657. The first pineapple to be grown in England was some twenty years later. Gardener John Rose presented Charles II with the pineapple in the garden of Dorney Court, near Eton. A painting depicting the event hangs in Ham House in London.

Pineapple culture on a large scale does not seem to have started until 1718 when Mr H. Telende, gardener to Sir Matthew Decker of Richmond in Surrey, was reported to be growing forty fruiting plants. Mr Telende grew them in pits built of brickwork, heated by 300 bushels of fermenting bark. He used a thermometer to make sure the temperature was correct, and it is probably from this date that thermometers and hygrometers became thought of as garden instruments.

As well as being grown in pits, pineapples could be grown in houses, the pots holding the plants plunged into beds of fermented leaves or tan on top of hot-water pipes. By the 1860s and 1870s, pineapple culture was at its peak. Most large estate gardens had a fruiting house, a similar house for succession, and a small house to bring on suckers.

Cheap imports eventually brought the 'noble pine' as an ornament to the tables of others than the rich. Although the flavour of home-grown pines is reputed to be legendary, judging by our own experiences, the gastronomic delights of Queens, Smooth-leaved Cayennes, Charlotte Rothschilds or any other of the twenty select varieties once grown in Britain, is likely to remain a memory.

Smooth-leaved Cayenne pineapple (left) and a pine forcing pit

It could be argued that grapes really aren't part of the kitchen garden but as most vineries were built within the garden walls and came as equally under the head gardener's critical eye as the vegetable plots, it seems fair to give an account of them. For reasons of economy the vines at Chilton had been pulled up in 1974 and, although we attempted pineapples, there was no way that a large and instant vine could be miraculously reinstated.

The nineteenth-century obsession with vines is, however, worth recording:

There is perhaps no plant the culture of which occupies so much of the attention of horticultural writers as the Vine. The soil in which it grows, the air in which it breathes, the system of training that should be adopted, whether its roots should have artificial heat or not, and many other questions connected with its culture, are discussed from week to week in all the horticultural periodicals of the day.

wrote William Thomson, editor of the *Gardener* in 1869.

And according to another publication there was: 'no plant which so soon shows the results of unskilful management or so well repays the grower for liberal treatment and any special care bestowed on it'.

This special care and liberal treatment started with the making of the vine border, an art in itself. In making a border, drainage was the key. Stones or bricks were put down first and drainpipes laid not only parallel to the border but across it to pass through the wall of the vinery via a small specially-built archway. Often with its roots in an outside border, this archway was the entry point of the vine into the vinery. Recommended for laying on top of the drainage material was three inches (8 cm) of friable old pasture which had been stacked for six months and then mixed with ground bones, charred earth or wood ashes. To this was added lime rubble and fresh horse droppings.

There could be whole ranges of vineries, variously known as Early, Middle or Late, their designation depending on the time at which each house was 'started', the term used when heat was applied in the house to prompt the vines into growth. Grapes to be ready in August had to be started off in January and the following-on second house started in the middle of February. Early grapes were forced by bottom heat from four rows of four-inch (10-cm) hot-water pipes which could give a heat of 60 degrees Fahrenheit (16°C), especially if the border was covered with dry leaves. On outside borders the leaves were often thatched with straw to throw off the rain. A careful balance had to be struck between applying enough heat to activate the vines but not so much that it burnt the roots.

It is hardly surprising that vines took up so much literature when you consider the amount of work which went into their maintenance. In the winter resting period, the vines had to be untied from their overhead wires to be trained into shape and pruned for greater vigour. There were several ways of doing this. The 'long rod' system was practised almost exclusively during the first half of the nineteenth century. The method involved training-in a number of young vine rods and pruning them so that the rods bore the fruit. The system was not so straightforward as the later-introduced spur pruning and, under careless management, the bearing rods could get crowded together and a great quantity of useless wood be produced. The 'short rod' system was the training of short rods instead of long ones. The 'extension system' allowed one vine to grow to fill a large house by itself. In this way it could produce a crop far greater than several vines occupying a similar space. The famous old Black Hamburgh vine at Hampton Court is trained on this system. In 1985 it produced 890 pounds (403 kilograms) of grapes. During the latter part of the nineteenth century the spur system became the most popular. By this method separate vines could be confined to a single stem by cutting back buds close to the stem. Each stem could then be trained up the sloping rafters of the vinery roof.

Black Hamburgh vine grown on the 'extension' system

In addition to pruning, painstaking scraping had to be done to remove all the loose bark from the vine and all the rods washed and inspected for insects. It is a method still employed by Dennis Hopkins at Chatsworth. During the winter months his gardeners scrape the vine barks in his early and late vineries. In Victorian times the vines were then tied down in large bow shapes to make them sprout evenly when it was time to start the house again. Once re-tied and re-started, work began again. First with disbudding (removing buds not needed), then thinning out (taking out unneeded shoots), followed by stopping (pinching off the end of the remaining shoots just above the joint due to bear the bunch) and finally, thinning the bunch itself so that it formed a pleasing shape – a careful art.

Grape gatherer

To obtain a house of healthy grapes a head gardener had to avoid mildew, rust, scalding, shrivelling and sometimes, if nourishment were not sufficient, shanking. Another hazard was grape cracking, caused by too much water being applied to the roots of the vine either naturally or artificially at the wrong time. Sometimes a vine might be wounded accidentally when the sap was rising and this made it bleed. The force at which a vine could bleed is illustrated by the following account given in John Lindley's *Theory of Horticulture*. A Mr Braddick writes of an experiment he carried out:

On the 20th of March, in the middle of a warm day, I selected a strong seedling vine five years old, which grew in a well-prepared soil, against a south-west wall; I took off its head horizontally with a clean cut, and immediately observed the sap rising rapidly through all the pores of the wood, from the centre to the bark. I wiped away the exuded moisture, and covered the wound with a piece of bladder, which I securely fastened with cement, and a strong binding of waxed twine. The bladder, although first drawn very close to the top of the shoot, soon began to stretch, and to rise like a ball over the wound: thus distended, and filled with the sap of the vine, it felt as hard as a cricket ball: and seemed, to all appearance, as if it would burst. I caused cold water from a well to be thrown on the roots of the plant; but neither this nor any other plan that I could devise, prevented the sap from flowing, which it continued to do with so much force as to burst the bladder, in about forty-eight hours after the operation was performed.

One remedy to stop the flow of sap when an accidental cut was made, was to mix four parts of scraped cheese to one part of calcined oyster shells and press the mixture strongly into the pores of the wood. This was popular until the advent in 1869 of 'Thomson's Styptic'. What was in Mr Thomson's compound is not known but it is highly probable that he was one and the same person as the before-mentioned William Thomson, editor of the *Gardener*, and a celebrated grape grower.

Mr Thomson became embroiled in a very 'sour grapes' incident in the same year as his Styptic was introduced. That year, at the Hamburg

International Horticultural Exhibition, Queen Victoria offered a silver cup to be awarded to the best three bunches of distinct sorts of grapes. Inspired by the thought of winning a cup offered by the Queen of England, several British growers entered. William Thomson was one and a certain Mr Meredith, another. Mr Thomson sent his son to Hamburg 'at great expense' with three bunches of grapes weighing thirteen pounds (5·9 kilograms). However, at the last minute officials changed the wording of the rules of entry to 'a collection' of grapes, not 'three bunches'. Angry British gardeners believed that the gentlemen of Hamburg had changed the wording so that one of their own countrymen could win the cup. Luckily Mr Meredith had taken enough bunches to quickly make up a collection and beat the Germans at their own game, securing the cup for himself. When Mr Thomson's son telegrammed the result to his father, Mr Thomson senior was highly indignant, particularly when reports reached him that his grapes had been superior to the ones shown by Mr Meredith. He immediately dispatched a letter to the secretary of the exhibition saying that in all the principles of fair dealing and common honesty, he protested against the change of wording, claimed the Cup and would accept no other prize but the Queen's Silver Cup. What reply the Germans gave is not known but Mr Thomson may have got off lightly, for gardeners who had actually made the trip to Hamburg had been compelled to pay an extortionate eighteen shillings (90p) entrance fee and, to add insult to injury, many had their plants or cuttings stolen.

It was an achievement to grow and show grapes successfully and quite another achievement to keep them once grown.

The preservation of grapes through the winter with the least amount of trouble is one of the most important of all matters to the British grape grower. Every cultivator, young and old, knows to his cost what a task it is to keep grapes hanging all winter after they are ripe.

So wrote the horticultural journalist William Robinson. Mr Robinson then proceeded to outline a solution to the problem.

He had recently been to France to study and report on French horticulture. When he visited Baron Rothschild's gardens at Ferrières he saw the Baron's manager, M. Bergman, cutting off bunches of grapes from vines but leaving a portion of the vine shoot attached like an umbilical cord to each bunch. M. Bergman put the shoot protruding from the bunch into a narrow-necked bottle which had previously been filled with water laced with charcoal to guard against impurities. The bottle was then placed to lean out at an angle from a specially designed wooden rack. Six to seven rows of bottles, each bottle containing a bunch of grapes, were placed one above the other to form high walls of hanging grapes. A space wide enough to walk up was left between each wall of grapes. Mr Robinson reported: 'I am told by experienced French growers who have adopted the system, that they keep the fruit as long this way as upon the vine with fewer mouldy berries and almost without trouble.' He recommended his readers to try the method, and by 1872 reports were appearing in the *Journal of Horticulture* of British gardeners keeping vines successfully in bottles of water. Mr John Potts of Heaton Grange, Bolton, wrote to say that on 10 February he had cut from his vine the last bunches of Alicante grapes that had ripened the preceding August. He then placed the shoot from each bunch into bottles of water and these grapes kept successfully until 12 May, the same day on which he cut his first new grapes. Mr Potts declared: 'The old grapes were nearly as handsome as the new, despite their having been ripe for nine months, six on the vine, and three in the bottles.'

The pigeon-holed racks which once lined grape store rooms have long since been pulled down and the rooms are used for other purposes today. However, remnants of the racks and a few grape storage bottles, particularly the later ones with their swan-shaped necks and central hole for topping-up water, can still be found.

The gargantuan business of nineteenth-century vine culture had an important lilliputian branch practised by skilful gardeners for modish employers. In an age when flowers and plants were imprisoned, pressed, trained, arranged and observed with an obsessiveness never since equalled, and when wired arches, yuccas, crotons, conifers, ornamental grasses, fuchsias and palms were *de rigueur* for dining-room table decoration, the quintessential refinement sought by hosts was a miniature living vine rising from the centre of their dining-room table – a vine complete with growing bunches of grapes at which guests could delicately pick.

There were two ways in which a gardener could obtain vines growing in pots small enough to suit this living dessert. One was to

22 (right): Bunches of grapes could be kept fresh for as long as three months after picking, by storing them in bottles of water sweetened with charcoal

Table-top vine

23

24

23 *Ripening Blenheim
Orange melons, safely
cradled in individual nets.
Above all things, per-
fection was required of
the Victorian melon*

24 *Syringes and fumi-
gators were necessary
weapons against insect
predators in the glasshouses*

25 *The cucumber house
and cucumber glasses. The
glasses were designed to
encompass growing fruits
and keep them straight*

26

26 *Apples and pears just picked and on their way to be stored in the thatched fruit house*

27 *Selection of dessert apples grown in the garden (from top, left to right): Devonshire Quarrenden, Blenheim Orange, Ribston Pippin, St Edmund's Pippin, Worcester Pearmain, Ashmead's Kernel, Pitmaston Pine Apple (the tiny one), Cornish Gilliflower, American Mother and Cox's Orange Pippin*

28 *Selection of pears grown in the garden (from top, left to right): Doyenné du Comice, Durondeau, Easter Beurré, Souvenir du Congrès, Louise Bonne of Jersey, Dr Jules Guyot, Conference, Fertility, Pitmaston Duchess and Bellissime d'Hiver*

29 *In the fruit house apples are better 'keepers' than pears. One way to test a pear's ripeness is to gently press the flesh around the stalk*

27

28

30

31

30 Harry digs up the cardoon which was to be sent up to London for the Royal Horticultural Society show

31 Root vegetables stored in sand

32 Early Horn carrots, like all root vegetables, were washed before being taken up to the kitchens

33 Mauve coloured kidney beans, an old variety

34 Harry displays baskets of vegetables and forced salading which were available from the garden in late winter

35 Baskets delivered to the kitchen on Christmas morning provided the cook with vegetables, fruits and herbs for the main meals and sufficient salading to accompany cold suppers

32

33

34

35

36 *Harry has made sure the fruit on the Christmas dining table is arranged to its best advantage and 'dressing' the table with flowers and greenery laid between the dishes. This skill, practised by his Victorian forebears, was handed down to the last generation of old-style head gardeners*

put an iron rod beside an ordinary-size vine when it was started into growth. The iron rod had a ring attached to it big enough to support a six- or eight-inch (15- or 20-cm) flower pot. As the vine rod grew, the gardener slipped a pot into the holder, manoeuvred the rod up through the bottom of the pot and trained it over a wire frame fixed in the pot. When the buds broke on the rod, all those below the pot were rubbed off and only the buds above the pot kept. These buds were stopped when they reached seven or eight inches (18 or 20 cm). Soil was then put into the pot and a trailing fern or other suitable greenery planted on its surface. The pot then filled with roots. When the grapes were ripe the cane below the pot was cut through by degrees, by which time the vine had established itself as a small pot plant.

The other method of achieving the same end was to place a large pot vine on a shelf and train it horizontally, putting five-inch (12-cm) pots filled with soil beneath it. The vine started to root into the pots and the shoots which were destined to bear the bunches of grapes were trained upright and cut away when they were fully rooted.

One would have thought that obtaining a miniature vine was achievement enough to satisfy the mistress of the house. However, for the nineteenth-century hostess the appearance of the vine in the dining-room heralded its own particular problem of etiquette. Apparently, living vines along with slender palms and elegant ferns 'should spring in gentle curves from the snowy cloth just as if they were growing unrestrained in their native habitat'. This necessity brought about a burning issue which filled many columns of the *Journal of Horticulture* during the 1870s. Should holes be cut in table tops or not? By cutting a hole into a table top, a pot could be safely sunk and concealed on a lower layer of the table leaving its contents to grow 'naturally' out of the snowy cloth. Owners of valuable mahogany tables were understandably touchy about cutting holes in them. Cutting holes in best damask tablecloths for 'let-ins' wasn't utterly warmed to either! An expensive alternative was found, at least for the table. The mahogany top was substituted by an ordinary deal top with a hole already cut into it. When the table was covered by a cloth, guests were unaware they were not sitting at mahogany. How the cloth problem was resolved is not known.

Although it is a long way from vines and even longer from kitchen gardens, it is worth recording the excesses to which table decoration went. In June 1873 a dinner table in New York had down its centre, in addition to banks of moss and several hundred yellow roses: 'a tank full of water, over which was an aviary of song birds, and in the midst of the water two live swans swam about, the whole being adorned with superb flowers, water lilies and ferns.'

A living vine, even had it withstood the attentions of the swans, would have hardly been noticed!

CHAPTER THIRTEEN

•

*Produce hampers – Tomatoes – Salutary tales of
cucumbers and melons.*

THE building in which Harry kept his van at the garden was a
spacious creosoted lean-to. Originally it had only one entrance,
at the opposite end to which the double garage doors were
now hung. Now home to a blue Fiat, the lean-to had also once held a
very different sort of conveyance, or perhaps more properly, forms of
conveyance, for before being known as the garage, it was called the
Black Shed and before that it had been known as the 'Hamper House'.

'Every fruit has to be perfectly ripe and ready for immediate use
when packed for a gentleman's table' was a nineteenth-century maxim.
In order to meet it, every head gardener had a supply of wicker hampers
which were brought into use to keep the family, when living in their
town house, supplied with fresh produce from their country estate.

Until the 1950s, a pony and cart carried produce hampers from
Chilton gardens to Hungerford station. The hampers were loaded
aboard the nine o'clock London train and arrived at the kitchens of a
house in Belgrave Square by noon.

A couple of old hampers were still perched on the rafters of the pot
shed. One had a leather label attached to its handle, the London address
on one side and the gardens on the other. When the hampers were
empty the label was simply turned round and the hampers sent back to
Hungerford station to be collected and refilled.

There were long hampers for flowers and separate square hampers
for fruit and vegetables. The only fruit that was put into the vegetable
hamper was cooking apples or pears. The kitchen garden foreman
picked the outside produce and packed the vegetables but the fruit boxes
and hampers were always packed by the inside foreman supervised by
the head gardener. Root vegetables were washed and put into the
bottom of the hamper. On top of these went the more solid vegetables,
such as heads of cabbages and cauliflowers. Next came peas and beans
and, on top, tender salading such as lettuce and tomatoes. Before the
hamper was strapped down, the contents were topped with a covering
of spinach. This was the vegetable least able to withstand any crushing
and putting it on top also provided a cushion for the other vegetables
packed in beneath.

*Harry demonstrates the
art of packing a vegetable
hamper*

Carefully preserved in Harry's fruit house were other, much smaller boxes. Harry explained that these were the sort of boxes that at one time every old, well-established garden would have had. These fitted inside the fruit hamper. One box lined with felt would hold twelve peaches. There was a removable cushion of bleached wadding to put on top of the fruit. Dessert plums and gages were also packed in a peach box, each fruit in a leaf or tissue paper and no more than a single layer to a box. Pears for eating uncooked were put in another box and packed almost as carefully. The first line went one way, then the next the other, so that the tops slotted into each other as neatly as a jigsaw.

There was a ten-inch (25-cm) square box with a depth to match one good strawberry or fig. Into this had gone fourteen ounces (400 grams) of best strawberries, each berry wrapped in a strawberry leaf and packed tightly enough to stop any movement and subsequent bruising but not so tightly that the berries were crushed. The skill required to pack a hamper properly was, said Harry, a closely guarded and handed-down secret. He himself had learned by watching his old head gardener, Uncle Fred Norris.

That this was so was borne out in a surprising way. An article found in the *Journal of Horticulture* for 1873 and entitled 'Packing Fruit for Travelling' confirmed that the rules by which Harry packed hampers and the design of the various fruit boxes had not changed for over a century.

The article went into great detail over the minute care to be taken in packing. It advocated that each fruit be looked over and cleaned with a soft brush, except in the case of fruit covered with bloom such as plums or black grapes. If possible, fruit was to be picked one or two days in advance and laid in a dry place to lose its 'superabundant humidity'; the materials for packing had also to be thoroughly dried. There was an addition to Harry's method of packing peaches. A bed of bran or good dry white sawdust from which the finer dust had been sifted, was first to be placed into the peach box. Once in place, the peaches themselves could also be covered with another layer of bran, the box being gently shaken so that the bran settled and left no crevice unfilled. Grapes were packed in the same way but had to be perfectly dry so that the bran or sawdust could be blown off. Cherries were to be washed in a basin of water with a soft brush, wiped dry and laid between two sheets of tissue paper before being packed in alternate layers of tow.

The various fruit boxes were recommended to be made of softwood but not deal, for deal had a 'certain resinous odour' which might have affected the natural perfume of the fruit. For winter travelling, the fruit boxes were protected from frost within the hamper by a three-inch (8-cm) covering of moss or straw kept in place by matting.

In July of 1887 the firm of Webber, fruit salesmen of Covent Garden, set up a competition for which they offered a prize of ten guineas (£10.50). The competition was to show 'the best mode of packing fruit for market or elsewhere, so as to enable it to arrive at its destination in the best condition'. Three packed boxes of fruit had to be delivered by the railway companies at South Kensington intact, in the way of ordinary parcels, consigned and signed for as customary.

The winner of this competition was William Crump, at that time head gardener at Blenheim. He packed his fruit on the 'Coleman System', so named because it was devised by Mr Coleman, head gardener at Eastnor Castle near Ledbury in Herefordshire. This method was to pack grapes on a bed of moss lined with tissue paper, with the same packing surrounding the sides of the box. The peaches were wrapped first in tissue paper then in wadding and placed closely on a bed of wadding. Strawberries were packed in a flat box in one layer and each strawberry wrapped in a mulberry leaf.

It is an interesting fact that of all the awards William Crump received (and there were many, including a first-class certificate for his famous melon, Blenheim Orange, more of which later) and considering he was one of the first men to receive the prestigious Victoria Medal of Honour in Horticulture, when interviewed in later years, Crump always claimed his most appreciated award was the one given by Webber's for their fruit packing competition. In fact, he won the competition twice in succession.

Above the spot where the rhubarb forcing pots had been was a short row of coldframes. Painted and reglazed, several of these were now successfully nurturing a crop of green capsicums and a small but healthy crop of purple egg plants. Harry had grown the egg plants as a matter of course but doubts set in. Were we being historically correct in having them as part of a nineteenth-century vegetable garden? Surprisingly, we were. The egg plant had been introduced into Britain as far back as 1597 to be cultivated for its fruit. There was another interesting fact which emerged from research. Of the several ways of cooking it, our ancestors had to overcome a problem we wouldn't think about today. When roasted on a gridiron and soaked in butter spiced with herbs, the succulence of the egg plant could be ruined by smoke from the fire. It seems the only way of getting round the problem was to cook the fruit between two plates.

Egg plants, like the tomato, were also grown for salads and flavouring, although the tomato itself was thought to have the additional

Below: Long and round capsicums, and egg plant

benefit of making an admirable sauce and green pickle. The tomato increased in popularity to a greater extent and more rapidly than any other vegetable during Victoria's reign. As late as the 1860s, however, one garden writer obviously felt that readers still needed reassurance over the culinary value of the tomato: 'Those who have analysed its properties say that the tomato is singularly wholesome, and very useful, especially in cases of bad digestion. It is still not appreciated or cultivated as it ought to be.'

This reluctance to eat tomatoes might well have stemmed from the fact that the plant's foliage and flowers bear a striking resemblance to the poisonous weed Deadly Nightshade, and although the 'Love Apple' (as it was first called because of its alleged aphrodisiac powers) was grown as an ornamental climber and curiosity, it did not become popular as a crop until well into the nineteenth century.

The Large Red and the Yellow seemed to be the preferred culinary varieties, while others, listed by Mme Vilmorin-Andrieux as 'large, small, round, red, yellow, wrinkled and swollen', were grown merely as novelties. Vilmorin-Andrieux also lists an Apple Shaped Purple, a large variety which turned almost violet when ripe. Checks with modern catalogues revealed that the Red Cherry, introduced in 1862, the Yellow Cherry, introduced six years later, the Yellow Pear shape and Red Currant are still being sold, although in some cases as an ornamental mixture rather than as separate varieties. Best of All, introduced in 1895, was also still being requested by some people although its popularity had fallen off over the past few years.

In addition to the Deadly Nightshade factor, British weather might well have put many gardeners off considering tomatoes as a crop. Before

Below (left to right):
Yellow cherry, yellow pear
and red currant tomatoes
Right: Wooden shading
and winding mechanism

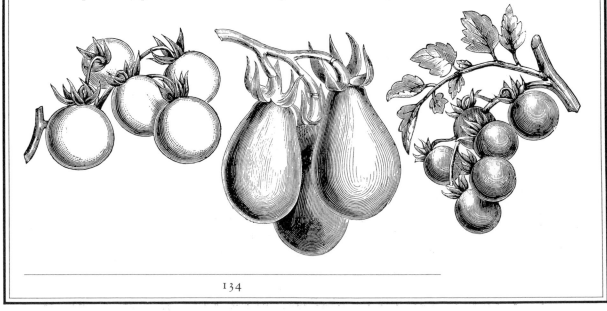

the advent of tomato houses, low-roofed roomy structures, specially erected in some large establishments towards the end of the century and in which tomatoes, given the right temperature, could be had all year round, the best way of ensuring a crop was to plant tomatoes against the sunny south wall of the garden. As we had no conveniently heated tomato house at Chilton we were bound to follow the old method of cultivation. At the end of May young plants were set out in the spaces between the nectarine and peach trees at the foot of the south wall fully exposed to the sun. If any cold nights came the plants would have to be covered with a few boughs. Too much growth and not enough early tomatoes had to be discouraged by 'stopping' the leading shoots on each plant. As each plant grew it had to be trained like its peach tree neighbour, with the shoots spread out against the wall and secured by loosely fastened shreds of bast tacked into the wall with a nail so that the fruit caught the full benefit of the sun.

At the same time as the tomatoes were planted, cucumber seeds were sown. The variety was Telegraph; these were thought to be equally sensitive to sun but in quite another way. Two large squares of thin, wooden-lathed blinds, grey with age, but quite complete, arrived by lorry. Also in the lorry, strapped to the sides, was a long wooden pole, what looked like two large iron fishing reels and a brass and green-painted watering barrel on wheels.

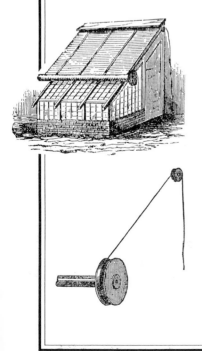

The lorry had been on a round trip: first to Kew Gardens to pick up the watering barrel and the iron fishing reels. These, with the pole, turned out to be blind-winding equipment from a demolished Victorian greenhouse and had been hunted out, dusted over and placed in a pile for us to borrow. Back on the M4 a similar kind loan had been rolled and was waiting in the gardens at Windsor Castle: two squares of wooden blinds, long unused and Victorian in every sense of the word. After unloading and considerable trial and error, the top pole, winding equipment and blinds were married together over the cucumber half of the cucumber/melon house. Once planted on their bed of manure in the house, the cucumbers, Harry warned, would need careful watering and airing.

'Giving air' was one way of keeping a step in front in the battle to keep the temperature constant in a cucumber house. If the thermometer showed signs of rising dangerously, opening the house at intervals could keep the temperature down. Harry's warnings about temperature changes were backed up by the old instruction manuals. A particularly dangerous time could be when bursts of sunshine followed dull, close weather. Shirley Hibberd pressed the point home in *The Amateur's Kitchen Garden* by telling the following salutary tale.

A proud owner had a span-roofed cucumber house 'clothed from the ground to the ridge line on both sides of the roof with gigantic vines, from which were suspended hundreds of cucumbers, the straightness and freshness of which were simply marvellous'. The man sent out a special invitation to his friends to view the cucumber house. A few days before the visitors were due to arrive the weather was dull, so the man's gardener kept the cucumber house closed. In the dullness there were, however, occasional bursts of sunshine. These sent the temperature inside the house up to 150 degrees Fahrenheit (65 °C) and, on the morning of the day the visitors were expected, when the owner opened up for a preliminary inspection: 'the great leaves hung like rags, the plants appeared as if cut through over the roots, and hurrying to that bourne from whence no cucumber returns'. The owner, being a quick-witted fellow, hastily ordered mats to be put on the outside of the roof to subdue the light inside and a coat of green to be smeared inside the roof to dim things still further. He next instructed that the plants be syringed until they were drenched and when this was done, locked up the house, gave the key to the gardener and told him to go to London and not come back for twenty-four hours. When the guests arrived, the owner explained that unfortunately his gardener had gone to London with the glasshouse key in his pocket but everyone was quite welcome to look through the glass. This they did, were apparently satisfied with what they saw and carried their host's fame as a cucumber grower 'with great noise round the world'.

The skill of growing cucumbers could begin even before they were sown. Old seeds were believed to produce plants which were much more luxuriant and fruitful than plants raised from new seed. If a head gardener could not obtain old seed he gave new seeds an artificial 'ageing' by carrying them around in his waistcoat pocket.

As can be gauged from Shirley Hibberd's tale, cucumber houses were seen as useful and ornamental. There were one or two cucumber varieties grown which had an entirely white outer skin or a light cream colour which apparently gave 'the fruit a remarkable appearance'.

Above: Rollisson's Telegraph cucumber
Below left: Cucumber leaves and flowers
Below right: Melon leaves and flowers

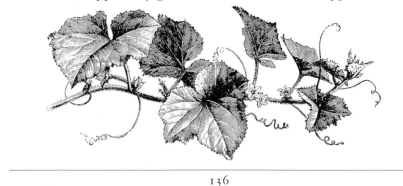

Something else, which although acceptable in Victorian days, would have given the fruit a remarkable appearance to modern eyes, was the practice of growing each cucumber in a glass tube to keep it straight. These tubes were either sold by mail order or could be bought from dealers in horticultural requisites. The danger of using these glass tubes was that during the swelling of the fruit it could become wedged tightly in the glass and not be able to be drawn out. A safer method was to nail three pieces of deal together to form an open-ended box three inches (8 cm) wide and deep and fit that over the growing cucumber.

The cucumber, like the tomato, was not a uniformly loved product of the nineteenth-century vegetable garden. Whereas in some places cucumbers were required for as long a period as possible, necessitating the gardener planting them successively in September and November so as to have fruit ready for cutting through winter as well as summer, in other places the cucumber was viewed with suspicion. Remarks were made about its bitter unwholesomeness and toxicity, particularly when left to hang too long before cutting. Pro-cucumberarians replied that anything that was 90 per cent water could not possibly be pernicious.

Harry top-dressed the old variety of Telegraph twice and the heaps of manure under each plant spread out to form a bed along the top of the greenhouse staging. Economic Victorian gardeners dibbled cuttings of Sweet Williams and Veronicas into their cucumber beds but our Telegraphs were sight enough in themselves. Harry had trained them to hang from a wire. Amongst their companions an experimental half-a-dozen gleamed strangely in their glazed straitjackets. Syringing and care paid off: one week there were fifty to sixty fruits hanging waiting to be cut and, after they had been cut, the same amount was ready in the following week.

Beneath the cavern of dark-green stalactites the cucumber half of the glasshouse had pleasingly turned into, the vista was impressive. With the central dividing door open the house, viewed from the doorway at the far end, turned into arches of shade hung either side with green, golden and net-patterned melons.

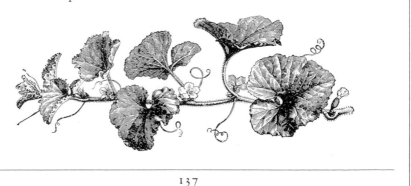

Viewing from the outer door was recommended not only for its pleasing aspect but for the sake of comfort. On warm days the syringing and liquid manure created a rather tropical clamminess beneath the succulent ramblings. The melons did not need as much water as their neighbouring cucumbers and Harry sprinkled a ring of yellow flowers of sulphur round the stem of each. This acted as a fungicide and caked to form a protective layer which water fell away from, preventing the stem lying damp. Each melon seedling had been planted on a single turf which had been turned grass side down on to the glasshouse staging and topped with a firm layer of fine soil or 'crumb'. Apart from when they were first planted out, at which time the old books recommended two or three rhubarb leaves being laid on the overhead glass for a few hours every day, the melons needed little shading. In fact, they needed the sun to bring them to perfection. Above all things, perfection was required of the Victorian melon.

Judging the correct time to cut a melon was a critical art. Ideally it should be cut when one or all of the following symptoms became apparent: the beginnings of a change in colour, parting from the parent stalk, the surface beginning to crack slightly and the fruit starting to give off its peculiarly rich aroma. Once cut, a melon had to be kept in a dry fruit room for a few days before being taken to the dining-room. If it was required to keep it longer, it could be stored in the ice-house.

Placing a melon on the dining-room table at exactly the right time to sample its perfection was a risky business. All the care in its culture could be rendered useless if the gardener was shamed by the melon being sent away from the table. The ignominy occasioned by such a happening was keenly felt by 'J.W.' writing in the *Journal of Horticulture* in 1877. Recounting his experience as a lesson to other gardeners, he explained that on nurturing a particular melon as an intended entry at an exhibition he had been annoyed to receive a message on the night before the exhibition that there was an important dinner party and the 'very best melon' was demanded for the table. He had no option but to cut and send his intended exhibition specimen. Next morning half of the melon was handed back with the damning comment 'not good'. 'J.W.' came to the conclusion that he had been at fault by cutting the melon when it was too ripe, it was, shamefully, one day too old. Taking a lesson from the experience, he cut another melon, from which the aroma was hardly noticeable, and entered that in the exhibition. The melon won first prize. Continuing the practice of cutting his melons before the 'aroma appeared to be fully developed', 'J.W.' was able to report that not one fruit was afterwards found fault with during the entire season.

Above: One of our Blenheim Orange melons Right: A golden melon, Hero of Lockinge, starting to smell distinctly ripe

Owing to the need for sun to bring the fruit to its perfection, the earliest a well-flavoured melon could be obtained was May, although very occasionally by putting plants in pots in a vinery or pinestove, ripe fruit could be produced in April. Once the season got under way, particularly at establishments where pineapples were not grown, there could be an almost daily demand for melons as dessert both summer and autumn. To meet the demand, head gardeners had to have as many as half a dozen houses planted up in succession.

With the melon being recognised as the 'noblest production' of the kitchen garden it was especially gratifying for head gardeners to experiment with producing their own varieties and enter them in competitions. The names of melons bespoke their origins: Frogmore

Blenheim orange. Augt 1880

Scarlet, Longleat Perfection, Oulton Park Hybrid, and Eastnor Castle. Exhibited successfully in 1880 against thirty other varieties, was a highly perfumed, oval-shaped melon with a 'netted' skin and orange-coloured flesh. The melon had been grown by William Crump, head gardener at the time to the Duke of Marlborough at Blenheim Palace, and was appropriately entered under the name of Blenheim Orange. Following on its success in competition, the melon was awarded a first-class certificate by the Royal Horticultural Society. Over a hundred years later only Blenheim Orange, together with a variety named Hero of Lockinge and a melon which originated from America in 1886 called Emerald Gem, appear to have survived. All three, the pale honey-coloured Hero of Lockinge, the green Emerald Gem and the patterned globe-like Blenheim Orange, hung in our melon house.

The fruits nearest to the bed were carefully supported on upturned pots, their companions higher up the stem nestled in individual, twelve-inch (30-cm) square hammocks, tied to an overhead wire. The hammocks, or melon nets as they are more properly called, are now as rare as hen's teeth. Our supply had come from the same source as the slatted wooden shading and a few more, if needed, had been promised by one of Harry's retired head gardener friends.

Above: Photograph from William Crump's own album showing Blenheim Orange melons in a melon house at Blenheim Palace Right: Cardoon

CHAPTER FOURTEEN

•

On using a wimble – The Great Autumn Show, present and past –
Concerning the qualities of fruit.

TOWARDS the end of summer a pungent musty smell began to percolate through the melon house. Several Blenheim Orange began to split away from their parent stems and Harry looked at them speculatively. One in particular looked as though it might be worth entering in the Royal Horticultural Society's Fruit and Vegetable Show which was to be held in October at Vincent Square in London.

The cardoon crop also came under scrutiny for the show. There were about a dozen cardoons, their stems ranged from four to five feet (1·2 to 1·5 metres) in height and their tops hung over with huge grey-blue indented leaves vaguely resembling giant celery heads. Before showing, the monstrous stalks would need to be blanched exactly as they would have been to fit them for the kitchen. The traditional and effective way of doing this is to wrap and tie a band of rolled hay round each stem from the base to the leaves.

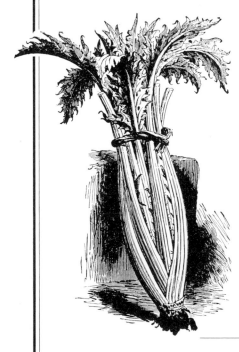

Harry had been taught to make a hayband in 1936 when he was at Stansted Park. The gardeners used to cut the grass for the haybands themselves, choosing grass at least a yard (1 metre) high which would make bands up to six feet (2 metres) in length. In the Stansted tool house there had been a wimble. This was simply a hook on a crank and looked like the brace part of an old brace and bit. When the grass had dried, the wimble was used to make the hayband. It needed two people. One person dipped into the pile of hay, wrapped the first length round the end hook and started twisting the crank, backing away from the haypile as he twisted. The other person stayed beside the haypile and as the band grew kept up a steady feed of hay.

Harry had neither the advantage of a proper wimble nor yard-long hay. The only hay available came from a bale cut by modern methods on the estate farm. For the wimble Harry converted a wheelbrace left over from the days of his van-before-last.

On a dry day, the hay was shaken into a heap on the pathway by the garden's double door. Harry operated the wimble, walking backwards along the garden path and working up a nice

steady twist, while Alison fed as evenly as she could the growing umbilical which stretched between them. Completed bands were heaped into a cardboard box and wheeled down to the cardoons. Enough bands had been made, once wrapped and tied, to cover comfortably (well, certainly cosily) six cardoons. In three or more weeks, in time for the show, the stems beneath the haybands should be whitened and sweetened.

Alison and Harry making haybands for the cardoons

Before the show there was an important point to clear up. The show schedule had no class for cardoons. Carrots, cabbages, marrows, onions, potatoes, tomatoes, turnips, yes – but no cardoon class. It needed a telephone call to the show's entry secretary to clear the matter. Well, he had never, in his time as secretary, had cardoons entered before, in fact he wasn't sure what they actually were. Obligingly a description was furnished as to their length and breadth, with the assurance that only one would be entered. The slightly shocked pause reverberating back down the phone after the explanation was dangerous. It seemed opportune to suggest quickly that perhaps the cardoon might fit into Class 126 reserved for 'Any other vegetable including pumpkins and gourds, not named above'. After a moment's thought this was agreed, provided that a large enough space could be made on the exhibit table. Thus the cardoon became officially committed to venture out into the show world again.

The evening before the show was calm and golden. A dapple of shade spread down from the hazel thicket across the door of the fruit house. On a shelf just inside the doorway – dark-green skins covered in cream cross patterns like contoured globes – were four Blenheim Orange melons. Three were cushioned on nests of tissue paper and one, bottom-end down, swelled from a small round wicker basket. Harry lifted and tentatively pressed the base of each melon, eventually choosing not the prize guy in the basket but one of the others which wasn't quite so ripe. This was the one to be tissue-papered and boxed for its journey to London.

Down in the centre of the garden two cardoons looked, despite their enormous size, white and vulnerable as the haybands were peeled away. Laid head forward in the elm wheelbarrow, thought to be a fittingly grand and antique conveyance, an avalanche of large leaves overflowed them and became wrapped round the iron wheel, making progress difficult although stately.

The melon, wrapped, boxed and tied with string, made a neat square parcel. The selected cardoon, washed, trimmed and wrapped in yards of tissue paper with bands of string drawn tight at head and foot, would not have looked out of place at the bottom of an Egyptian sarcophagus.

It was generally agreed that Harry could not possibly cope on the early morning commuter train with the mummified cardoon and that Alison should drive to London with it that evening and stay overnight at a hotel near Shepherd's Bush. The cardoon, for fear of wilting in the heat of the hotel, stayed outside, balefully propped up in the back seat of the car. Alison spent an anxious night dreaming of car thieves but the vegetable proved intimidating and remained safe and unwilting on the parking meter.

It was particularly fitting that Alison should attend the Fruit and Vegetable Show for, according to our Victorian edition of the *Horticultural Exhibitors' Handbook*, exhibitions were 'valuable object lessons to the aspiring and uninitiated tyro, forming an excellent medium for learning what could be attained towards perfection in horticulture by a diligent application of skill and industry'.

The *Handbook* recommended that all exhibitors set their specimens in 'the most perfect condition attainable' with 'all the tasteful effect which their skill and experience could devise'. Laying the cardoon tastefully proved taxing, there was not much one could do except give it a pleasing perimeter of table top by furtively moving away the

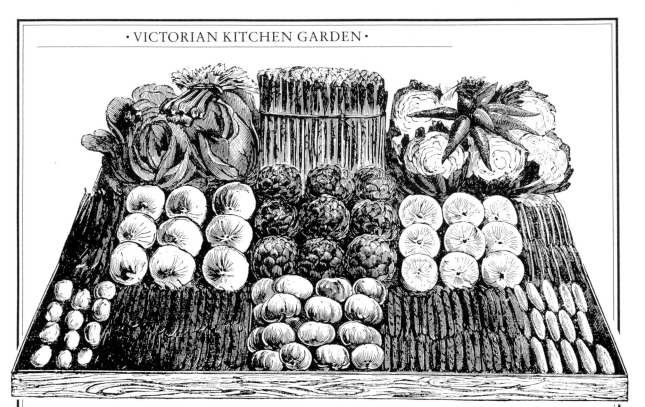

First-prize collection of fifteen varieties of vegetables, from the Amateur's Kitchen Garden, 1877

surrounding pumpkins from either side. The melon was fairly simple to set. It was just placed on a white plate on a central exhibit table. It looked lonely but self-sufficient. There was competition in the Melon Class – two others, one worryingly large.

On green hessian display panels running above green hessian-covered tables and on rows of trestle tables which stretched like long ribs across the vast hall, other exhibitors had employed their 'tasteful skill and experience'. Giant onions perched on blocks, glowing and spherical as Kremlin domes, weighty green cabbages with leaves like elephant ears stretched in formidable lines, and against the hessianed walls 'collections' of nine different vegetables spread, flanked either side by long white leeks whose tops billowed and tapered like vertical Spirits of Ecstasy.

There were plates of apples, culinary and dessert; dishes of pears, of quinces and of nuts. Next to the three melons was the Grape Class. It had two entries, and each competitor had pinned shapely twin bunches, bloom unsmudged, on to a sloping white-papered display stand. In the centre of the hall apples rose scarlet and shiny from wicker baskets each divided by yellow quinces. In the middle of this central table was a display stand which stood higher than all the rest. It had dishes of apples around the base, in the middle and on the top.

Sun struck through the wide-vaulted glass roof and, viewed from a high side window, the tables in the hall below stretched like strips of red and green mosaic. If it looked impressive today how must it have looked a hundred years ago when not one, but many, and much higher, stands rose not only from the central table but from tables all round the hall? Stands displaying six melons, each melon dish hung around with bunches of grapes and with melons and peaches on dishes around its base. Stands with thirty apples to a dish, eight dishes to a stand, the highest dish topped by palm fronds and the central stem of the stand wrapped round with ferns and shadowed by hanging bunches of grapes.

How must it have looked when the old fruit nurseries set displays which had a central pyramid built of hundreds of apples topped by palms or a quartet of pineapples? When there were not just two entries of grapes but rows of white display boards, three bunches to a board and some bunches weighing seven and a half pounds (3·4 kilograms) or more. How splendid Mr Rivers' miniature fruiting vines in pots must have looked and the displays of oranges, lemons and bunches of bananas, brought to a rich yellow colour, their proper state for exhibition. In those days when a head gardener set his display he knew that a pineapple took the most marks, followed by the grape, then the melon and, in descending order, the peach, nectarine, fig, apricot, pear, plum, cherry, apple, strawberry, raspberry and currant. He knew that amongst dessert fruit, rich flavour, high quality and pleasing appearance had to prevail and that every culinary fruit had to be large, useful, of even outline and fine flavour.

Victorian high standards and ideals did however suffer from a temporary scandal. It was the lure of the handsome melons which was the problem. In the days when every competitor had a favourite variety which he cultivated with much diligence and success, saving seed from home-grown melons was better than buying seed. It was also the seed from successfully exhibited melons which formed the basis for 'sending out' new melon varieties. All the honour and profit from this achievement could be seriously marred if anyone surreptitiously pilfered the seed which, sadly, in 1868 the judges did, according to correspondence in the *Journal of Horticulture*.

It was inconceivable that such kleptomaniac tendencies would be found in today's judges who, summoned by a hand-rung bell, were sent off in pairs, the fruit men to the right, the vegetable experts to the left. While the weighing, sniffing, cutting and contemplation went on inside, outdoors a taxi-fed queue stretched from the flag-fluttering entrance down towards Victoria station.

As soon as judging finished, the crowds were let in while judges and other officials migrated upstairs for more business. The Royal

Left: Royal Horticultural Society judges at the turn of the century

Horticultural Society was founded in 1804 at the suggestion of John Wedgwood, son of the famous potter Josiah Wedgwood. Its aim was to 'collect every information respecting the culture and treatment of all plants and trees, as well culinary as ornamental'.

One way of furthering that aim was to set up various committees, one of which was the Fruit Committee which met on the first Monday of every month. At its inception in 1858, the business of the Fruit Committee was laid down to be:

Examining and reporting upon all fruits or esculents brought under their notice, collecting information concerning the qualities of the fruits grown in different parts of the United Kingdom, and advising the Council generally as to the best modes of increasing the Society's power of promoting the improvement of Fruits and Esculents cultivated in Great Britain and Ireland.

Now, almost 130 years on, that committee, known today as the Fruit and Vegetable Committee, was to continue with its tradition of a monthly meeting to examine and report on new fruits.

Harry is a committee member and he and fellow members sat at tables arranged in a horseshoe shape at the toe of which sat the chairman and the secretary. The committee is a careful cross-section of men representing a wide span of experience. There are head gardeners, who like Harry have spent their lives attaining excellence on private estates; respected nurserymen of many years' standing and members of staff from government research stations such as Long Ashton and East Malling. Each committee member is furnished with a white plate and a knife (the latter often redundant as a variety of bone-handled, worn-bladed instruments appeared from pockets at the appropriate moment).

On the left-hand side of the committee room a table was set with plates of fruit, some from the Society's trial grounds at Wisley. These were new varieties being monitored which are brought at intervals before the committee for them to pronounce on progress. Some are foreign varieties, this year Japanese pears, more savoury than sweet, and an apple from Sweden in its second year of trial. Other fruit comes from the government research stations, while yet more dishes contain fruit sent in by proud and hopeful members of the public. Every grower aspires to produce a specimen as popular and tasty as a Cox's Orange Pippin.

In a formal ritual a student from Wisley stands beside the fruit table and, upon the chairman's instructions, picks up a dish of fruit together with a card containing details of the contents. He walks with the dish in one hand and the card displayed for reading in the other. First he approaches the chairman's table and then makes his way round the inside of the horseshoe offering each committee member a fruit from the dish while displaying the card. With a clatter and rattle of plates the fruit is spliced, tasted and talked about. Its texture, flavour, appearance, cropping season, culinary suitability, resemblance to other varieties and manageability all come under discussion.

Some fruits meet favour but need more time on trial. Members of the public are voted to be politely thanked for their samples even when these – unfortunately – have not turned out to be the stunning new varieties their owners hoped. Others, more lucky, might be invited to send a graft from their tree or bush to Wisley for extensive trials to see if the fruit might have commercial value or, if it should be a biannual cropper, be useful for small gardens. Varieties eventually considered worthy are given to selected, experienced nurserymen to propagate and the Society shows dishes of the fruit at its autumn exhibitions. Any interested member of the public is given the name of a nursery where the fruit is available.

With business completed, the committee rises, is thanked for attending, wished a good lunch by the chairman and disperses, leaving a line of plates piled high with cores and different coloured peel.

Meanwhile in the hall downstairs the cardoon is occasioning interest. A perplexed couple from Portsmouth contemplate it for some time. The wife thinks it looks like celery at one end and fennel at the other. They read the label hesitantly and agree they have never seen a vegetable like it before. It is too large for their garden – they have just about enough room for tomatoes. Another lady sniffs it and comments to her friend that it looks like a thistle. The friend, not one to mince words, thinks it looks a bit rough!

At around three o'clock an official comes down into the hall and starts propping cards against the winning exhibits. He comes near the pumpkin table and puts a Third Prize ticket on to the cardoon, surprising the lady who preferred her vegetables on a more delicate scale.

Anxious approaches to the table where the Blenheim Orange melon is reveal no card propped up. Close to, a white square comes into view, lying flat beside the plate – it's the First Prize ticket. Harry is there beaming at Alison, there's nothing to stop a good small one beating a good big one, especially when the quality's right. He explains that perhaps the loser may have been picked a bit late. Maybe a day too late? The prize money will be sent on, together with the certificate.

In 1862 the First Prize was £1 10s od (£1.50), now it's gone up to a giddy £3. But it's not the money that counts, it's the honour of winning First Prize at the Royal Horticultural Show. William Crump of Madresfield and Blenheim would have been pleased too.

CHAPTER FIFTEEN

•

Fruit gathering and the importance of the fruit house –
Entombing nuts – Storing vegetables and making
a Christmas basket.

INSIDE the crumbling green covers of the *Book of Garden Management* we found the encouraging opinion that 'fruit-gathering is one of the most cheerful and agreeable employments connected with garden management'. Already fragile when purchased, almost twelve months of constant use resulted in the cover parting company from the text. Fragility apart, the book was sound enough in comment. Fruit-gathering *was* agreeable.

In the early part of the year the thatched fruit house had been scrubbed out ready for the first of the soft fruits ripening in July and August. Peaches, nectarines, sweet cherries, plums and gages were only short-stay visitors on the fruit-house shelves. Years ago, most soft fruits would have been picked at six in the evening and taken straight up to the mansion for dinner that night. Harry remembered using the house as a way to build up a stock of strawberries, often necessary if large dinner parties and special occasions came together. Instead of leaving the berries untouched and over-ripening in the hot sun, he picked each day, putting the berries carefully in the house where they kept fresh for a number of days.

Peaches and nectarines, once they gave off that certain 'translucence' Harry associated with ripeness, were cupped in the hand and given a slight twist. Coming away from the stalk easily they were turned over and placed on to padded trays. Nectarines were looked at carefully and taken off when just ripe to avoid the sun scalding their thin skins.

A fruit which traditionally never saw the inside of the fruit house was the dark red morello cherry. The bunches hanging down in clusters against the north wall were stripped of their berries, leaving the stalks on the tree. Small beads of juice around the top of each where the stalk had come away made it necessary to send them at once, in white tissue-lined boxes, to the housekeeper for preserving.

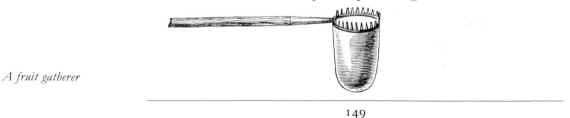

A fruit gatherer

Early apples, such as the beautiful smooth green and speckled Irish Peach; the small Beauty of Bath and vivid scarlet Worcester Pearmain, winner of a Grand Exhibition First Class Certificate in 1874, would each for ease of watching have been placed in one layer on the fruit-room shelves. They are not 'keepers' and are best eaten straight from the tree. The delightful but diminutive crops borne by our very young trees looked better left on the trees anyway, giving as they did a splash of colour along the rails and wires on the terrace above the coldframes.

Larger crops of early fruit came on the old pear trees which had been in the garden at the time the restoration project started. Clapp's Favourite, an antique American variety, ripened first, then the musky smelling Jargonelle and succulent William's *Bon Chrétien*. These were pears which were always appreciated for their early appearance on the dining-room table but, like the early apples, they would not keep.

The straw wadding was taken out of the fruit-house window in late September in preparation for gathering the bulk of the fruit. For dessert apples there were Cox's Orange Pippin, Blenheim Orange, Cornish Gilliflower, Ashmead's Kernel, Ribston Pippin, American Mother, Egremont Russet, Devonshire Quarrenden and the tiny yellow Pitmaston Pineapple. Valued for its lateness and flavour was the yellowish-green and russet Sturmer Pippin. Lastly, valued unfortunately only for its lateness, was the Wagener, an apple introduced in 1796 but, perhaps because its flavour is considered disagreeable by most people, not even mentioned in Hogg's comprehensive *Fruit Manual*.

For culinary apples there were Lane's Prince Albert, Bramley's Seedling, Lord Derby, Warner's King, Newton Wonder and Golden Noble.

Picking the apples was relatively easy. With the trees trained as espaliers and cordons, most of the fruit was within hand reach. If the branches had been less accessible it might have been worth making and trying out one of the nineteenth-century fruit gatherers recommended. It was a device which looked like a bathbrush with no central bristles and a circumference of pegs standing in for the outer edge of bristles. The principle was to pass the fruit-bearing branch through the pegs and comb the fruit off, holding it safely captured inside the upturned circle of pegs.

Gathered safely by hand, all the apples were placed in double layers on the slatted fruit-house shelves. Harry said that when he'd been at Stansted Park, the old fruit foreman had wrapped every apple separately in a piece of greased paper before stacking it. Perhaps this kept in the moisture. In former days, however, moisture and choice pears were kept well apart. The *Book of Garden Management* recommended gathering them precariously by their stalks, avoiding all hand contact which

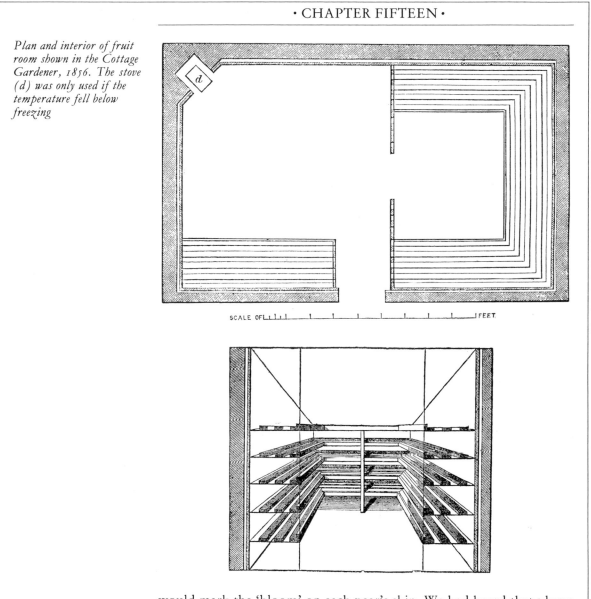

Plan and interior of fruit room shown in the Cottage Gardener, 1856. The stove (d) was only used if the temperature fell below freezing

SCALE OF ⊢⊢⊢⊢⊢⊢⊢⊢⊢⊢⊢⊢⊢⊢⊣ FEET.

would mark the 'bloom' on each pear's skin. We had heard that plums had been gathered in baskets lined with nettles to avoid smudging their bloom but avoiding contact with the not so obvious bloom on pears was an interesting idea. The theory was that, kept preserved, the bloom would mean that the pear would never need wiping and would keep its flavour and freshness. Harry said that the care taken in gathering fruit in the past was far greater than is taken today. Young journeymen and improver journeymen were never allowed to do the picking, their job was to hold the basket for the fruit foreman.

Picked on dry days, like the rest of the fruit, were the mid-season dessert pears. Beurré Superfin; Beurré Hardy and Louise Bonne of Jersey. At the end of October, Pitmaston Duchess was ready and the 'ornamental' (as Hogg described it) Durondeau. Harry thought Durondeau a pretty pear, but no good otherwise, certainly not to be compared with the Doyenné du Comice. Hogg described Doyenné du Comice as rich, sweet and delicately perfumed with an almost cinnamon flavour. Harry called it the finest dessert pear there is, worth a grower going to no end of trouble to get to perfection and the best pear a man could put on his employer's table. However, he said the pear could be an embarrassment as well-dined guests might not want an enormous pear for their dessert.

Emile D'Heyst with its rose-water perfume followed the Comices, and three late pears were the Glou Morceau, Easter Beurré and white gritty Catillac. The Catillacs hung on as hard as turnips until late October and would keep in the fruit house until next May. Also late were a few Conference trees trained as oblique cordons against the north wall. The cool position of these stretched the Conference's season from mid-September through to the end of October.

Easter Beurré pear

With the straw removed from the window the cool nights lowered the temperature inside the fruit house. When it was down to 40 degrees Fahrenheit (4°C) the straw went back in and the outer and inner door were shut and locked. To avoid decay, the temperature was kept as constant as possible and we went into the house as little as possible. Some Victorian gardeners even went to the lengths of having canvas curtains hung on rollers, dropping the canvas down in front of the shelves to keep out air and light every time it was necessary to open the house.

Amongst all these fruit varieties there was a sad omission. It would not have fruited anyway, but it should have sprouted a hopeful leaf or two – it didn't. The Maltster apple graft made in March looked what it was, remarkably dead. It had fallen victim to a spell of cold, wet weather in early summer and quietly expired. Had it, in fact, ever actually 'taken' at all? From the twig-like remains it was difficult to tell. A ray of hope lit the despondency. The parent tree still flourished in the National Apple Collection. Whilst it lived, the opportunity to encourage Maltster progeny (allowing for the right weather and degree of enthusiasm) would remain.

Nuts gathered from the filbert thickets which enclosed and stretched to right and left of the fruit house, were gathered in baskets. To keep the husks, the open baskets were left to stand for a night and shaken to evacuate the tenant earwigs. The *Book of Garden Management* said that the best method of preserving filberts was to pack them in glazed earthenware jars, sprinkle a little salt over the last layer and tie down the tops with coarse brown paper. The jars then had to be kept in a damp cellar. Effective though this might have been, it provided us with difficulties, not the least being the lack of a cellar. We eventually followed Harry's suggestion which was to revive the method used by his predecessor, Mr Beckett, at the turn of the century. This was simply to bury two seakale pots in the ground beside the fruit house. Each pot rested on a tile with the pot rim sunk six inches (15 cm) below ground level. Once filled with nuts, the lids went back on to the pots and the ground was levelled above them. Spread with the surrounding sprawling ground cover of ivy and small fallen branches, the burial place, even though it was outside the safety of the walled garden, was as undetectable to passing opportunists as a lost Pharaoh's tomb.

Filbert nut

All the coldframes holding vegetables still growing or being blanched had now to have their lights lifted regularly. This was needed to give the plants beneath an airing to prevent moulds and mildew forming. Several sheaves of combed wheat straw were purchased from a thatching company near Newbury. The straw was to be made into mats to cover the coldframe lights before the first frosts came. In 1862 suitable sheaves had been 'tenpence a fathom of six bundles', today they worked out at £2.50 a sheaf.

Laid completely flat and propped up waist high, an old glassless coldframe top served as a loom, giving a flat surface to work across and a guide to the exact measurements the mats had to be. Alison stood inside the makeshift loom with the sheaf propped beside her. Drawing out of the sheaf a bundle of straw about $1\frac{1}{2}$ inches (4 cm) thick she laid it flat across the frame and tied it in three places with three separate pieces of tarred string, leaving the strings trailing uncut. These strings then secured the next bundle and so on until the bundles stretched in succession to cover the whole frame. Even with practice each mat took a day to finish, but once completed they looked, and there is no better word, beautiful. Harry had suggested that the wheat ears be left on the straw and the stalks laid so that the ears from the two bundles met in the middle of the mat. In the garden and unrolled on to the coldframe tops, the mats caught the evening sunlight and glistened like flattened gold nuggets.

Years ago a head gardener would have been able to send his staff to fetch a plentiful supply of bracken from the Wild Garden, in the pleasure grounds, our supply had to come from a particularly shady roadside verge. Harry cut it whilst it was still green, for had it been left until it turned brown, the fronds would have fallen off and it would have been useless for the job for which it was intended – frost protection. The bracken was laid out to dry in the old rose house and tossed at regular intervals. When it was dry enough, some was thatched around the surviving cardoons, other pieces over the globe artichokes and, following an old manual and by way of an experiment, the remainder was thatched over a line of hooped hazel sticks covering a row of celery. The principle behind the bracken and hoop method was to prevent alternate frost and wet rotting the celery heads. If this happened, a good part of the celery had to be cut away before sending it to the table.

Shallots were lifted, dried and tied on a string in descending pairs. They hung in a disused glasshouse. The same glasshouse also provided cover and a drying place for the everlasting sea lavender, Acroclinium and Rhodanthe which had been picked from the flower borders flanking the garden's central walkway.

The unheated old show house, briefly colourful during the summer months, was now forced to return to bare staging. Its most exotic inhabitants, a collection of Japanese chrysanthemums with blooms bigger than a man's head, were loaded carefully on to the wooden handbarrow and carried away to finish their days in less romantic but warmer surroundings. The ancestors of these extraordinary giants had been brought back from Japan by Robert Fortune in 1846. Regarded by the Victorians as curious and 'showy', the striking colours and massive blooms were considered highly attractive and much grown for decorating conservatories and show houses. Today, rather like the Gloucester Old Spot pig, they have fallen out of favour for being too gross and, like the pig, become almost extinct.

All the root vegetables were gradually lifted. They were piled in partitioned heaps and covered with dry sand in the root store. As with the fruit, they would have to be checked over on wet days. Patches of ground which had looked small when filled with growing vegetables seemed mysteriously to widen in size when empty. Rows of brassicas planted together in the central vegetable plots ameliorated the surrounding emptiness. Wide bluish-green January Kings stood in lines beside fat, round, dark-red pickling cabbages. Brussels sprouts clustered with buttons rose behind white and purple sprouting broccoli. Beyond the broccoli was Scotch kale, as attractive with its bright green plumes as the purple and cream streaked rosettes of nearby garnishing kale. Less flamboyant, but valued now as much for their contrast in leaf formation as taste, were neighbouring rows of leeks and spinach.

Manure from the spent hotbeds was wheeled on to the empty plots.

Parsnip

It was a hopeful gesture, maybe the plots would grow crops again next year, maybe not. The winding down process of the garden had begun and, with the end of the project approaching, there was no forward beating rhythm of tasks to alleviate it.

Harry stacked some chicory in a cool place ready for forcing as a Christmas crop, but there was no need now to look further ahead. No need to chill rhubarb and seakale crowns for forcing to fill the hungry gap which always began a new year. It was traditionally the time to repair broken panes of glass and faulty doors but the glasshouses stood empty and the cosmetic repairs made an autumn ago had worn too thin to resuscitate.

Before the severe frosts set in, Harry lifted a few prime cauliflowers and, with the balls of damp earth still wrapped around their roots, hung them head downwards in a dry shed. We now had an abundance of vegetables in store: scorzonera, salsify, shallots, onions, beetroot, potatoes, turnips, parsnips and carrots. The brassicas, leeks and Jerusalem artichokes could safely be left in the garden. In order to keep it for garnishing, a square of parsley was covered with a lantern handlight.

As December drew to a close, Harry made up a Christmas salad basket. From the coldframes came young carrots, radishes and blanched endive. From under a bell cloche, tender Lamb's lettuce and from beneath lantern handlights came speckled Bath Brown Cos. There was forced crisp chicory and there was celery but, alas, the celery measured up not at all to its salad companions. The hoop and bracken method had preserved its head wonderfully but the stalks below hung like strips of Gruyère cheese. With a wet summer on their side, slugs had slid through the protective layer of sifted coal ashes and lime and had been alternately feasting and blessing nineteenth-century pest control for some considerable time.

Eminent men speaking at Queen Victoria's Jubilee celebrations in 1897 considered the achievements in horticulture made during the sixty years of her reign to have been as rapid and far-reaching as any attained in industry, arts or sciences. If, during the brief period of our experiment at turning the clock back, we had gone some way in recording this, together with an echo back from the walls of the bounty and excellence kitchen gardens once provided, and if we had managed to rekindle the skills of the men who had once worked within those walls, then despite losing the Maltster and the celery becoming raddled, our project had been a success.

BIBLIOGRAPHY

•

* indicates the book is out of print

BOOKS

Aikman, C.M. *Manures and the principles of Manuring* Blackwood and Sons, 1894*.

Beeton, S.O. *The Book of Garden Management* London, 1862*.

Bunyard, E. *Handbook of Hardy Fruits more commonly Grown in Great Britain* J. Murray, 1925*.

Cobbett, W. *The English Gardener* The author, 1829* Oxford UP, pbk 1980.

Dallas, E.S. *Kettner's Book of the Table: a manual of cookery, practical, theoretical, historical* London, 1877*, Centaur Press, 1968.

Delamer, E.S. *The Kitchen Garden or the culture in the open ground of roots, vegetables, herbs and fruits* Routledge, 1855*.

Dods, M. *The Cook and Housewife's Manual containing the most approved modern recipes for making soups, gravies, sauces etc.* Edinburgh, 1826*.

Hedrick, U.P. *The Small Fruits of New York* New York, 1925*.

Hibberd, S. *The Amateur's Kitchen Garden, Frame-ground and Forcing Pit* Groombridge, 1877*.

Hibberd, S. *Profitable Gardening: a practical guide to the culture of vegetables, fruits . . .* London, 1863*.

Hogg, R. *The Fruit Manual containing the descriptions and synonyms of the fruits and fruit trees commonly met with in the gardens . . . of Great Britain etc.* Journal of the Horticultural Office, 5th edn. 1884*.

Lindley, J. *The Theory of Horticulture or an attempt to explain the . . . operations of gardening upon physiological principles* London, 1840*.

Loudon, Mrs J. *Gardening for Ladies* London, 1840, and later edns*.

Mawe, T. *Everyman his own Gardener* W. Griffin, 1767, and later edns*.

Parkinson, J. *Paradisi in sole, paradisus terrestris* H. Lownes and R. Young, 1629*.

Rivers, T. *Catalogue of Roses . . . a descriptive catalogue of selected roses cultivated for sale* London, 1833*.

Rivers, T. *The Miniature Fruit Garden: or the culture of pyramidal fruit trees . . .* Longman, 1850*.

Rivers, T. *The Orchard House or the cultivation of fruit trees in pots under glass* London, 1851, and several later edns*.

Thompson, R. *The Gardener's Assistant, practical and scientific* Glasgow, 1859, and later edns*.

Vilmorin-Andrieux, Mme. *The Vegetable Garden* J. Murray, 1885; reprint 1977.

Williamson, W. *The Horticultural Exhibitors' Handbook* (revised by M. Dunn) Blackwood and Sons, 1892*.

Additional books referred to but not mentioned in text
Barron, A.F. *Vines and Vine Culture* Journal of Horticulture, 1883, and later edns*.
Oldham, C.H. *The Cultivation of Berried Fruits in Great Britain* Crosby Lockwood, 1946*.
The Fruit Yearbook Royal Horticultural Society, 1949*.

JOURNALS
The Journal of Horticulture; The Gardeners' Chronicle; The Gardener; The Cottage Gardener.

INDEX

•

Page numbers in italic refer to black-and-white illustrations

157